THE SIMPLE ART OF GLUTEN-FREE BAKING COOKBOOK

Satisfy Your Cravings With Delicious and Easy Recipes for Snacks, Bread, and Desserts; Featuring Allergy-Friendly and Dairy-Free Options

Andrew Rabbio

Table of Contents

Chapter 3: Cookies, Brownies, & Bars

Chapter 4: Bread

Chapter 5: Cakes and Cupcakes

Chapter 6: Tarts, Pies, Pastries, & Cobblers

INTRODUCTION

— •••••••• —

Welcome to *"The Simple Art of Gluten-Free Baking Cookbook"* — where scrumptious treats meet worry-free indulgence! Say goodbye to gluten and hello to a world of mouthwatering delights that'll leave you craving more. Get ready to embark on a gluten-free adventure that's packed with flavor and simplicity.

In this cookbook, we've curated a treasure trove of delectable recipes that will have you swooning over every bite. Whether you're a seasoned gluten-free guru or just beginning your allergen-friendly journey, we've got you covered! From delightful snacks that'll tickle your taste buds to breads that boast a perfect balance of softness and crunch, we've included a wide range of options to keep you happily munching.

Oh, and did we mention desserts? Prepare to be dazzled by an array of heavenly sweets that cater not only to your gluten-free needs but also to those who prefer dairy-free indulgence. Everyone deserves a slice of deliciousness, and we've made sure no one is left out of this scrumptious party.

So, let go of any baking anxiety you may have, as we believe in keeping it simple and fun! You don't need to be a master chef to whip up these extraordinary creations. With our easy-to-follow recipes and helpful tips, you'll be wielding your mixing bowl like a gluten-free pro in no time.

Get ready to tantalize your taste buds and impress friends and family with treats that not only look spectacular but taste absolutely divine. "The Simple Art of Gluten-Free Baking Cookbook" is your gateway to unleashing the joy of baking without gluten and allergens — because being allergy-friendly doesn't mean compromising on flavor!

So, tie on your apron, gather your ingredients, and let's embark on a delightful journey of gluten-free baking magic. Get ready to savor the joy of simple, scrumptious, and worry-free delights. Let's bake up a storm!

CHAPTER 1

Gluten-free Baking 101

What is Gluten?

Gluten is like the pesky glue that holds wheat, barley, and rye together, giving bread and other baked goods their elasticity. Unfortunately, it can be a troublemaker for those with celiac disease or gluten sensitivity, causing all sorts of discomfort. But fear not! We've got the secret to scrumptious baking without it.

Benefits of Going Gluten-Free

Say hello to a happier tummy and newfound energy! Going gluten-free can reduce digestive issues, boost your mood, and even improve nutrient absorption. Plus, it opens doors to a world of exciting alternative flours that bring unique flavors and textures to your baked goodies.

How is Gluten-Free Baking Different?

If you are used to using normal wheat flour in all your recipes then going gluten-free will definitely take some getting used to. The rules are different and sometimes you have to get creative with the ingredients to mimic the qualities of gluten in your favorite baked goods. The biggest difference you will notice when baking gluten free is the texture of your dough or batter. Gluten-free baking requires more liquid to hydrate the flours so often times your bread "dough" might look more like a bread batter, and that's perfectly normal.

The added moisture also helps give your creations more spring in the oven making fluffier breads and treats that have a more rich texture.

Tips and Tricks for Gluten-Free Baking Bliss:

Give it a rest:

Before your creations go into the oven make sure you let the dough or batter rest for a few minutes. This extra time allows the flours to fully hydrate and helps you avoid the dreaded dry, cardboard-like texture gluten-free baked goods have been synonymous with over the years.

Embrace xanthan gum:

This superhero ingredient adds the elasticity gluten usually provides, ensuring your bakes stay delightfully fluffy and cohesive.

Don't overthink it:

Gluten-free baking is all about experimentation and fun. So, don't stress if your first try isn't perfect. Learn from it and keep on baking!

Stay moist:

Keep your baked goods moist and tender with additions like applesauce, yogurt, pumpkin or even a splash of orange juice. Your taste buds will thank you!

Read before you knead:

Be sure to read through the entire recipe before you start. This will help you avoid silly mistakes and make the process much easier. Also try to avoid modifying the recipe the first time you make it. After you have achieved the desired result then you can play with modifications like different flavor combinations.

Make is Vegan:

In some recipes, it is mentioned to use flax egg as a substitute for egg. To make 1 flax egg, combine 1 tablespoon of ground flaxseeds with 3 tablespoons of water in a bowl. Let it rest for 15 minutes. You can place it at room temperature or in the refrigerator for resting. It will become gel-like give it a good stir before incorporating it in with the other ingredients.

Now that you're armed with the basics, let your creativity flow, and dive into the world of gluten-free baking! With a bit of imagination and a dash of enthusiasm, you'll whip up delights that'll impress even the most die-hard gluten fans. So, grab your apron, preheat that oven, and let's bake up some gluten-free magic!

Guide to Gluten-Free Flours and Flour Blends:

Gluten-free baking can be a bit of a puzzle, but fear not!We've got your back with this comprehensive guide to gluten-free flours. From the most common flours to crafting the perfect flour blend, get ready to elevate your gluten-free baking game!

Most Common Gluten-Free Flours

Rice Flour: A staple in gluten-free baking, rice flour comes in two varieties — white rice flour (milder flavor) and brown rice flour (nuttier taste). It's great for cakes, cookies, and bread.

Almond Flour: Made from ground almonds, this flour brings a delightful nuttiness to your baked goods. It's perfect for muffins, macarons, and crusts.

Coconut Flour: A high-fiber option with a subtle coconut taste, coconut flour absorbs a lot of moisture, so use it in small quantities or blend with other flours. Ideal for pancakes, waffles, and cookies.

Tapioca Flour/Starch: Derived from the cassava root, tapioca flour adds chewiness and elasticity to your bakes. Combine it with other flours to achieve a lighter texture.

Potato Starch: Light and airy, potato starch works wonders in cake and cookie recipes, providing tenderness and structure.

Flour Blends – The Perfect Mix!

Creating a well-balanced flour blend is key to achieving the best results in gluten-free baking. Each flour brings its unique properties, so mixing them up allows you to enjoy the best of all worlds. For many of the recipes we've kept it simple and told you exactly which store-bought flour blend will give you the best results. Other times we simply say "gluten-free 1:1 flour" which means any store bought brand that says 1:1 or cup for cup on the front will work. Not everyone has the time to make their own flour blends but if you want to give it a try here's a basic flour blend recipe to get you started:

Gluten-Free All-Purpose Flour Blend:

- 1 cup fine rice flour (white or brown)
- 1 cup potato starch
- 1/2 cup tapioca flour/starch
- 1 teaspoon xanthan gum (for added elasticity)

Instructions: Simply whisk all the ingredients together until well combined. Store in an airtight container, and you're all set to use it as a one-to-one replacement for regular all-purpose flour in your favorite recipes.

Pro tip: Feel free to customize your blend based on the desired texture and flavor of your baked goods. Experiment with different ratios of flours to achieve the perfect balance for your specific recipe.

Recomended Flour Blends
- Bob's Red Mill 1:1 flour: This blend is great for cookies, muffins, scones, and some breads as well
- King Arthur Gluten-Free All-Purpose Flour: This blend is great for pastries, pie ans tart crust, some breads and cobblers.

Can't Find These Brands?
No Problem, these brands are popular in the US and CA but other countries will have their own gluten free flours. Do some research and see what is available at your local store. Any rice based blend will work well for these recipes. Happy Baking!

Equipment List

Having the right equipment in your kitchen will make it much easier to follow any recipe in this book or try your versions of other recipes. Here is a list of equipment you should ideally have in your kitchen to make gluten-free baking easy:

- digital kitchen scale
- digital thermometer
- wire cooling rack
- large baking sheets
- muffin or cupcake pans
- measuring spoons
- mixing bowls
- liquid measuring cups
- silicone spatula
- hand mixer

- stand mixer
- metal balloon whisk
- rolling pin
- piping bags and decorating tips
- round biscuit cutters
- sifter
- loaf pan
- muffin or cupcake liners
- parchment paper sheets
- cutting board

CHAPTER 2

Muffins, Scones, & Quick Breads

Bakery Style Blueberry Muffins

Yields: 24 standard muffins   or   12 jumbo muffins

Ingredients:

- ⅔ cup (150g) butter, softened (or dairy free butter)
- 2 cups (400g) granulated sugar
- ⅔ cup (160g) plain yogurt (or non-dairy yogurt)
- 2 cups (480ml) whole milk (or milk alternative)
- ⅔ cup (150ml) melted, slightly cooled coconut oil
- 4 large eggs at room temperature (or flax eggs)
- 2 teaspoons (10ml) vanilla extract
- 6 cups (720g) gluten-free 1:1 flour
- 2 teaspoons (10g) ground cinnamon
- 2 tablespoons (30g) baking powder
- 3 cups (450g) fresh or frozen blueberries (do not thaw if frozen)

Nut-Free Dairy-Free Option, Soy-Free, Vegan Option

Directions:

1. Start by preheating the oven to 425 °F (220 °C). Grease muffin pans with cooking spray or line them with disposable liners.
2. Add butter, sugar, yogurt, milk, oil, eggs, and vanilla into a bowl and stir until well incorporated.
3. In a separate bowl combine flour, cinnamon, and baking powder. Gradually add the flour mixture to the wet ingredients and mix them together with a spoon or rubber spatula until well incorporated.
4. Gently fold in the blueberries until distributed evenly throughout the batter.
5. Distribute the batter equally into prepared muffin cups (about ¾ full).
6. Place the muffin pans in the oven and bake for 5 minutes at 425 °F (220 °C) then turn the temperature down to 350 °F (177 °C) and continue baking for 25–30 minutes or until lightly golden brown on top and a toothpick inserted in the center comes out clean.
7. Remove the muffin from the oven and allow them to cool in the pan for 10 minutes. Gently remove the freshly cooled muffins from the pans and allow them to cool completely on a wire rack. Store them in the fridge in a sealed container for up to 7 days or freeze them to enjoy later.

Pumpkin Oat Chocolate Chip Muffins

Yields: 24 standard muffins

Ingredients:

- 3 cups (360g) gluten-free rolled oats + ½ cup (120g) for garnish
- 2 teaspoons (10g) pumpkin pie spice
- ½ teaspoon (3g) salt
- 2 teaspoons (10g) baking powder
- ½ teaspoon (3g) baking soda
- 4 large eggs
- 1 ½ cups (330g) packed dark brown sugar
- 2 teaspoons (10ml) vanilla extract
- 2 cups (480g) pumpkin puree
- 6 tablespoons (90ml) canola oil
- ⅔ cup (160g) mini chocolate chips (or dairy free chocolate chips)

Nut-Free, Soy-Free, Dairy-Free Option

Directions:

1. Preheat the oven to 350 °F (177 °C). Grease 2 muffin pans of 12 count each with cooking spray or line them with disposable liners.
2. Finely grind the oats in a blender.
3. Add baking powder, baking soda, pumpkin pie spice, and salt to the blender or food processor and pulse until well incorporated.
4. Add brown sugar, pumpkin puree, eggs, vanilla, and oil into the blender or food processor and blend until well combined.
5. Pour the batter into a bowl. Add chocolate chips and stir until well combined.
6. Spoon the batter into the muffin cups, filling up to 3/4, and lightly top with gluten-free rolled oats. Bake at 350 °F (177 °C) for 18–20 minutes or until a toothpick inserted into the center comes out clean.

Carrot Cake Muffins

Yields: 24 standard muffins

Ingredients:

- 1 cup (200g) light brown sugar
- ⅔ cup (160ml) avocado oil or vegetable oil
- 4 large eggs
- ⅔ cup (160ml) applesauce
- ½ cup (120ml) maple syrup
- ½ cup (120ml) dairy or non-dairy milk
- 2 teaspoons (10ml) apple cider vinegar
- 2 teaspoons (10ml) vanilla extract
- 2 cups (200g) blanched almond flour
- 3 cups (360g) gluten-free 1:1 flour
- 2 teaspoons (10g) baking soda
- 3 teaspoons (15g) baking powder
- ½ teaspoon (3g) ground ginger
- ½ teaspoon (3g) ground cloves
- 2 teaspoons (10g) ground cinnamon
- ½ teaspoon (3g) ground nutmeg
- 1 teaspoon (5g) salt
- 1 cup (120g) chopped walnuts (optional)
- 2 ½ cups (300g) shredded carrots

For streusel topping:
- 6 tablespoons (90g) brown sugar
- 3 tablespoons (45g) softened butter or refined coconut oil
- 6 tablespoons (90g) gluten free 1:1 flour
- 1 teaspoon (5g) ground cinnamon

Soy-Free, Dairy-Free Option

Directions:

1. Start by preheating the oven to 425 °F (220 °C). Coat 2 muffin pans of 12 count each with cooking spray or line them with disposable liners.
2. Add sugar, oil, eggs, applesauce, maple syrup, milk, vinegar, and vanilla extract into a bowl and whisk until well incorporated.
3. In a separate bowl combine the flours, baking powder, baking soda, spices, and salt.
4. Add the flour mixture to the egg mixture and stir until well combined.
5. Add carrots and walnuts and stir well. You will have a thick batter.
6. Distribute the batter among the muffin cups, about ¾ full.
7. For the streusel topping: Combine flour, butter, cinnamon, and sugar in a bowl. Mix until the mixture is crumbly. If the mixture is too moist, add extra flour.
8. Sprinkle the streusel topping on top of the batter in the cups.
9. Place the muffin pans in the oven and bake for 3 minutes at 425 °F (220 °C) then turn the temperature down to 350 °F (177 °C) and continue baking for 12–16 minutes or until lightly golden brown on top.

Cranberry Orange Muffins

Yields: 24 standard muffins

Nut-Free, Dairy-Free Option, Soy-Free

Ingredients:

- 3 ½ cups (420g) gluten-free 1:1 baking flour
- 1 teaspoon (5g) salt
- 2 tablespoons (30g) baking powder
- 3 cups or 12 ounces' (340g) cranberries, fresh or frozen, chopped (do not thaw if frozen)
- ½ cup (100g) brown sugar
- 1 cup (200g) granulated sugar
- 6 large eggs
- 1 cup (225g) butter or vegan butter, melted
- ¼ cup (60ml) orange juice
- 1 cup (240g) full-fat, plain yogurt or vegan yogurt
- 4 teaspoons (20g) grated orange zest

For streusel topping:

- ½ cup (70g) gluten-free 1:1 baking flour
- 1 (5g) teaspoon ground cinnamon
- 1 cup (200g) granulated sugar
- ⅔ cup (150g) cold butter or vegan butter, cut into small cubes

Directions:

1. Preheat oven to 400 °F (200 °C). Grease 2 muffin pans of 12 count each with cooking spray or line them with disposable liners.
2. Crack the eggs into a mixing bowl. Add brown sugar, granulated sugar yogurt, orange juice orange zest, and butter, and whisk until well combined.
3. Combine flour, baking powder, and salt in a bowl. Add the flour mixture to the egg mixture and stir until well incorporated. Add cranberries and stir.
4. Cover the bowl with plastic wrap and set aside for 30 minutes. Make sure you do not skip this step.
5. For streusel topping: Combine flour, cinnamon, and sugar in a bowl Add butter and mix with your hands or a pastry cutter until crumbly.
6. Distribute the batter among the muffin cups, about ¾ full. Sprinkle the streusel topping on top of the batter.
7. Bake at 400 °F (200 °C) for 18–22 minutes or until golden brown on top

Oatmeal Raisin Muffins

Yields: 24 standard muffins

Nut-Free, Dairy-Free, Vegan Option, Soy-Free

Ingredients:

- 4 (480g) cups gluten free rolled oats
- 2 teaspoons (10g) baking soda
- ½ teaspoon (3g) sea salt
- 4 teaspoons (20g) ground cinnamon
- 1 1/3 cups (220g) raisins
- 2 cups (480ml) unsweetened applesauce
- 1 cup (240ml) pure maple syrup
- 6 tablespoons (90ml) avocado oil or melted coconut oil
- 4 large eggs (flax egg for vegan option

Directions:

1. Preheat oven to 350 °F (177 °C). Coat 2 muffin pans of 12 counts each with cooking spray or line them with disposable liners.
2. Add all ingredients except the raisins to a blender or food processor and blend until well incorporated and free from clumps.
3. Pour batter into a bowl and add raisins. Stir with a spatula until well incorporated. Spoon the batter into the muffin cups, filling them about ¾ full, and bake at 350 °F (177 °C) for 12–15 minutes or until a toothpick inserted into the center of the muffin comes out clean.

Double Chocolate Muffins

Yields: 24 standard muffins

Ingredients:

- 3 cups (360g) gluten-free 1:1 flour
- 2 teaspoons (10g) baking soda
- 1 teaspoon (5g) baking powder
- ½ teaspoon (3g) xanthan gum
- 1 cup (120g) cocoa powder
- 2 cups (400g) granulated sugar
- ½ teaspoon (3g) salt
- 2 teaspoons (10ml) vanilla extract
- 1 cup (175g) regular or dairy-free chocolate chips
- ⅔ cup (150g) butter, softened (or dairy free butter)
- 4 large eggs at room temperature
- 2 cups (480ml) of whole milk (or milk alternative)

Dairy-Free Option, Nut-Free

Directions:

1. Preheat the oven to 350 °F (177 °C) Coat 2 muffin pans of 12 counts each with cooking spray or line them with disposable liners.
2. Add the eggs, butter, sugar, vanilla, and milk to a mixing bowl and whisk until well incorporated
3. in a separate bowl combine flour, baking soda, baking powder, xanthan gum, salt, and cocoa powder. Pour the flour mixture into the wet ingredients and mix until no clumps remain. fold in the chocolate chips and let the batter rest on the counter for 5-10 minutes.
4. Spoon the rested batter into the muffin cups and bake at 350 °F (177 °C) for 20–25 minutes or until a toothpick inserted into the center of the muffin comes out clean.

Savory Breakfast Muffins

Yields: 24 standard muffins

Soy-Free, Nut-Free

Ingredients:

- 1 cup (120g) blanched almond flour
- 1 cup (100g) finely grated parmesan cheese
- ½ cup (60g) nutritional yeast flakes
- ½ teaspoon (3g) garlic powder
- ½ teaspoon (3g) onion powder
- ¼ teaspoon (1g) ground black pepper
- ½ teaspoon (3g) salt
- ¼ cup (30g) raw hemp seeds
- 2 tablespoons (15g) flaxseed meal
- ¼ teaspoon (1g) baking powder
- 12 large eggs
- ⅔ cup (160ml) thinly sliced green onions
- 1 cup (240g) reduced-fat cottage cheese

Directions:

1. Preheat the oven to 375 ºF (190 ºC). Grease 2 muffin pans (12 counts each) with some cooking spray, or line them with disposable liners.
2. Add almond flour, parmesan, nutritional yeast, garlic powder, onion powder, pepper, salt, hemp seeds, flaxseed meal, and baking powder into a bowl and mix until well combined.
3. Add cottage cheese and eggs into a bowl and whisk well. Stir in the green onions.
4. Add the flour mixture to the wet ingredients a little at a time, and whisk each time until well combined.
5. Spoon the batter into greased muffin cups, up to ¾.
6. Bake at 375 ºF (190 ºC) for about 20-25 minutes.
7. Store in the fridge in a sealed container for up to 7 days

Apple Cheddar Scones

Yields: 8 large scones

Nut-Free, Soy-Free

Ingredients:

- 2 cup (240) gluten-free 1:1 flour
- 1 teaspoon (5g) baking soda
- 1 tablespoon (15g) baking powder
- ½ teaspoon (3g) salt
- ⅓ cup (70g) brown sugar
- ¼ teaspoon (1g) xanthan gum
- ⅓ cup (75g) butter, frozen
- 2 large eggs
- ¼ cup (60ml) half and half
- ½ cup (120ml) sour cream
- ½ cup (60g) grated sharp white cheddar cheese
- 1 large granny smith apple, peeled, cored, and chopped into bite-size chunks
- demerara sugar to sprinkle

For the egg wash:

- 1 egg, beaten

Directions:

1. Place the apple pieces on a baking sheet and roast at 400 ºF (200 ºC) for about 15 minutes or until slightly dry. They should not be browned. Let them cool to room temperature.
2. Take out the butter from the freezer and grate the butter using the larger holes of the grater. Place it back in the freezer until you need to use it.
3. Combine flour, baking soda, baking powder, salt, sugar, and xanthan gum in a bowl.
4. Add frozen, grated butter to the flour mixture and stir well. Place the bowl in the refrigerator.
5. Beat eggs in a bowl then add half and half, sour cream, and cheese. Stir until well incorporated.
6. Turn up the oven temperature to 425 ºF (220 ºC) and let it preheat.
7. Add the egg mixture to the flour mixture and stir until just combined.
8. Add apples and stir. If the batter is very dry, add some extra half and half.
9. Line a baking sheet with parchment paper. Divide the dough into 2 equal portions and place on the baking sheet. Shape each into a circle of about 1 ½ inches thick. Leave a sufficient gap
10. Brush the egg wash over the circles, sprinkle it with demerara sugar, and place it in the oven. Bake at 425 ºF (220 ºC) for 10–12 minutes or until a toothpick inserted into the center comes out clean.
11. Cool for about 5–8 minutes. Cut into 8 equal wedges and serve warm or store in the fridge.

Vanilla Lavender Earl Grey Scones

Yields: 8 large scones

Ingredients:

- 2 cups (240g) gluten-free 1:1 flour
- 1 teaspoon (5g) baking soda
- 1 tablespoon (15g) baking powder
- 2 lavender earl grey tea bags
- ½ teaspoon (3g) salt
- ⅓ cup (70g) brown sugar
- 2 teaspoons (10ml) vanilla extract
- ¼ teaspoon (1g) xanthan gum
- ⅓ cup (75g) butter, frozen
- 2 large eggs
- ½ cup (120ml) half and half
- ½ cup (120ml) sour cream

For the egg wash:

- 1 egg, beaten

Nut Free, Soy-Free

Directions:

1. Open tea bags and pour them into a glass jar. Add half and half and sour cream to the jar and let it rest in the fridge overnight or for at least 4 hours.
2. Preheat oven to 425 ºF (220 ºC) and prepare a baking sheet lined with parchment paper
3. Take out the butter from the freezer and grate the butter using the larger holes of the grater. Place it back in the freezer until you need to use it.
4. Combine flour, baking soda, baking powder, salt, and xanthan gum in a bowl.
5. Add frozen, grated butter and stir well. Place the bowl in the refrigerator.
6. Strain the milk and tea mixture into a bowl and whisk in the eggs, vanilla, and brown sugar.
7. Add the egg mixture to the flour mixture and stir until combined. If the batter is very dry add some extra half and half.
8. Divide the dough into 2 equal portions on the prepared baking sheet. Shape each into a circle of about 1 ½ inches thick. Leave a sufficient gap
9. Brush the egg wash over the circles, sprinkle it with demerara sugar, and place it in the oven. Bake at 425 ºF (220 ºC) for 10–12 minutes or until a toothpick inserted into the center comes out clean.
10. Cool for about 5–8 minutes. Cut into 8 equal wedges and serve warm or store in the fridge.

Orange Cardamom Scones

Yields: 8 large scones

Ingredients:

- 3 ½ cups (420g) gluten-free 1:1 flour
- 4 teaspoons (20g) baking powder
- 3 tablespoons (45g) granulated sugar
- 1 ½ teaspoons (2g) ground cardamom
- zest of 1 orange
- ½ teaspoon (3g) salt
- 2 large eggs (or flax eggs)
- ½ cup (120ml) yogurt (or dairy-free yogurt)
- ½ cup (120ml) maple syrup
- ½ cup (115g) butter, chilled, cubed (or vegan butter)

For the glaze:

- 1 cup (125g) powdered sugar
- 2 tablespoons (30ml) orange juice

Vegan Option, Nut-Free, Dairy-Free Option, Soy-Free

Directions:

1. Combine flour, baking powder, sugar, cardamom and salt in a mixing bowl.
2. Add cubed butter and cut into the dry ingredients using a fork until only pea-sized lumps remain. Place the bowl into the fridge while you mix the wet ingredients.
3. Whisk together yogurt, eggs, maple syrup, and orange zest until well combined.
4. Add the flour mixture to the wet ingredients and mix well, there should still be clumps of butter in the dough.
5. Divide the dough into 2 equal portions and cover with plastic wrap. Place in the freezer until the oven is preheated.
6. Preheat the oven to 400 ºF (200 ºC). Place a sheet of parchment paper on a baking sheet.
7. Remove the dough from the freezer and unwrap them from the plastic. Place the dough balls on the baking sheet and shape them into about 1 ½ inch thick circles. Keep sufficient space between the circles.
8. Bake at 400 ºF (200 ºC) for 12-14 minutes.
9. Remove from the oven and allow them to cool completely on the baking sheet.
10. Meanwhile, make the glaze: Add powdered sugar, and orange juice into a bowl and whisk well until no clumps are present.
11. Cut each circle into 4-6 equal sections and transfer to a wire rack placed over a baking sheet.
12. Drizzle the glaze over the scones and allow time for the glaze to set. Store in the fridge in a sealed container to keep them fresh.

Savory Cheddar Chive Scones

Yields: 8 large scones

Ingredients:

- 2 cups plus 3 tablespoons (300g) gluten-free 1:1
- ¼ teaspoon (1g) baking soda
- 1 tablespoon (15g) baking powder
- 1 teaspoon (3g) garlic powder
- ¼ teaspoon (1g) xanthan gum
- ½ cup (60g) sharp cheddar cheese grated (or vegan cheddar cheese)
- ¼ cup (15g) finely chopped fresh chives
- 1 large egg (or flax egg)
- ¼ teaspoon (1g) salt
- 2 tablespoons (25g) granulated sugar
- 8 tablespoons (115g) butter or vegan butter, frozen, cubed
- ½ cup (120ml) sour cream or vegan sour cream
- ½ cup (120ml) buttermilk or whole milk (or non-dairy milk mixed with 2 teaspoons of lemon juice)

To top:

- 2 tablespoons (30g) butter, melted (or vegan butter)

Nut-Free, Soy-Free, Vegan Option, Dairy-Free Option

Directions:

1. Preheat oven to 425 °F (220 °C) and prepare a baking sheet with parchment paper
2. Combine flour, baking soda, baking powder, xanthan gum, garlic powder, salt, and cane sugar in a bowl. Add frozen butter and cut into flour mixture with a fork until only pea-sized lumps remain.
3. Add buttermilk, egg, chives, sour cream, and cheese into another bowl and stir until well combined.
4. Add the buttermilk mixture and mix well. If the mixture is very dry, add extra buttermilk, a teaspoon at a time, and mix well each time.
5. Keep the bowl covered in the refrigerator for about 15 minutes.
6. Divide the dough into 2 portions and shape into balls.
7. Place the dough balls on the prepared baking sheet and shape them into about 1 ½ inches thick circles. Keep sufficient space between the circles. Cut into 4 equal wedges and place them at least 1 inch apart then brush with butter, Place the baking sheet in the refrigerator for an additional 15 minutes if you are making vegan scones.
8. Place the baking sheet in the oven and bake at 425 °F (220 °C) for 12–13 minutes.
9. Keep the scones in the fridge in a sealed container if not enjoying right away.

Lemon Blueberry Scones

Yields: 8 large scones

Ingredients:

- 2 ½ cups (300g) gluten-free 1:1 flour
- ½ tablespoon (8g) baking powder
- ¼ cup (50g) granulated sugar
- ¼ teaspoon (1g) sea salt
- ½ cup (75g) fresh or frozen blueberries
- 10 tablespoons (150ml) full-fat canned coconut milk
- zest of 1 lemon
- juice of 1 lemon, strained
- 1 teaspoon (5ml) vanilla extract

Vegan, Dairy-Free, Soy-Free, Nut-Free

Directions:

1. Preheat the oven to 400 °F (200 °C). Prepare a baking sheet lined with parchment paper
2. Combine flour, baking powder, sugar, lemon zest, and salt in a bowl.
3. Stir in the coconut milk and lemon juice until dough forms and no clumps remain.
4. If the dough is sticky and does not form into a ball, add some extra flour, 1–2 tablespoons at a time and mix well each time.
5. If the dough is very dry, add extra coconut milk, a tablespoon at a time, and mix well each time.
6. Fold in blueberries until distributed throughout the dough.
7. Form the dough into a ball and place on a well floured surface. tt. Flatten the dough into a round of about 1 ½ inches thick.
8. Cut into 8 equal wedges and place them at least 1 inch apart on the prepared baking sheet.
9. Place the baking sheet in the oven on the center rack and bake at 400 °F (200 °C) for 20–22 minutes or until golden brown. Allow to cool on the baking sheet for 8-10 minutes

Lemon Poppy Seed Bread

Yields: 1 loaf

Ingredients:

- ¾ cup (180ml) avocado oil, extra-virgin olive oil, or melted coconut oil
- zest of 1 lemon
- 1 cup (200g) granulated sugar
- ¾ cup (180ml) unsweetened almond milk or any other non-dairy milk
- 3 large eggs, beaten
- juice of 1 large lemon, strained
- ½ teaspoon (2g) xanthan gum
- 2 cups (240g) gluten free 1:1 flour
- 1 teaspoon (5g) salt
- 4 tablespoons (40g) poppy seeds

Directions:

1. Preheat the oven to 350 °F (177 °C). Coat a loaf pan (8 x 4 inches with cooking spray.
2. Add oil, lemon zest, and sugar into a bowl and whisk well.
3. Whisk in the eggs, lemon juice, and almond milk. Whisk until the mixture is light in color.
4. Combine flour, baking powder, xanthan gum, poppy seeds, and salt in a separate bowl.
5. Combine the flour mixture and the egg mixture. Pour batter into the prepared loaf pan
6. Place the loaf pan in the oven and bake at 350 °F (177 °C) for 35-45 minutes or until the top of the bread is golden brown.
7. Allow the bread to cool for 10 minutes in the pan before removing it and transferring to a wire rack to cool completely.

Dark Chocolate Pumpkin Bread

Yields: 1 loaf

Dairy-Free, Soy-Free

Ingredients:

- 1 cup (240ml) pumpkin puree
- 3 tablespoons (45ml) melted coconut oil
- 2 large eggs
- ¼ cup (60ml) full-fat coconut milk
- ⅓ cup (80ml) honey or pure maple syrup
- 1 teaspoon (5g) vanilla extract
- 2 tablespoons (15g) golden flaxseed meal
- 1 ½ teaspoons (8g) pumpkin pie spice
- 1 teaspoon (5g) baking soda
- 2 cups (240g) blanched almond flour
- ¼ cup (30g) raw cacao powder
- ½ teaspoon (3g) salt
- ¾ cup (110g) coarsely chopped 70% dark chocolate (or dairy-free chocolate)

Optional mix-ins:

- chopped nuts like pecans or walnuts
- seeds
- dried fruits
- shredded coconut
- nut butter

Directions:

1. Preheat the oven to 350 ºF (177 ºC). Coat a loaf pan (8 x 4 inches each) with cooking spray.
2. Add pumpkin puree, coconut oil, eggs, milk, honey, and vanilla into a bowl and whisk until smooth.
3. Combine flaxseed meal, pumpkin spice, baking soda, almond flour, cacao powder, and salt in another bowl.
4. Add the flour mixture into the egg mixture and stir until you get a thick batter.
5. Gently fold in 3/4 of the chopped dark chocolate. Add any optional mix-ins if using, and fold gently. If you use nut butter, simply swirl the nut butter into the batter.
6. Pour the batter into the prepared loaf pan. Top with remaining chocolate.
7. Place the loaf pan in the oven and bake at 350 ºF (177 ºC) for 35-40 minutes.
8. Allow the bread to cool in the pan for 10 minutes before removing and transferring to a wire rack to cool completely.

Chocolate Zucchini Bread

Yields: 1 loaf

Nut-Free, Soy Free, Dairy-Free Option, Vegan Option

Ingredients:

- 1 cup (120g) gluten-free 1:1 flour
- 1 1/2 teaspoons (8g) baking soda
- ½ cup (40g) unsweetened cocoa powder
- 1 teaspoon (5g) baking powder
- ½ teaspoon (3g) salt
- ½ teaspoon (3g) xanthan gum
- 2 large eggs (or flax eggs)
- 1/4 cup (60ml) plain yogurt (or dairy-free yogurt)
- 2 teaspoons (10ml) vanilla extract
- 1/2 cup (85g) chocolate chips
- 1/4 cup (60ml) vegetable oil or melted coconut oil
- ¾ cup (150g) light brown sugar
- 3 cups (360g) shredded zucchini

Directions:

1. Preheat the oven to 350 ºF (177 ºC) Coat loaf pan (9 x 5 inches each) with cooking spray.
2. Add flour, xanthan gum, baking powder, baking soda, cocoa, and salt into a mixing bowl and stir well.
3. Beat eggs in another bowl then add yogurt, vanilla, oil, and brown sugar.
4. Add the egg mixture to the flour mixture and stir until well combined. You will get a thick batter.
5. Spread the shredded zucchini on a plate and pat the zucchini lightly with paper towels.
6. Add zucchini into the batter and stir until well combined.
7. Place the loaf pan in the oven and bake at 350 ºF (177 ºC) for 45–50 minutes or until a toothpick inserted into the center of the bread comes out clean.
8. Allow the bread to cool in the pan for 10 minutes before removing and transferring to a wire rack to cool completely.

Banana Walnut Bread

Yields: 1 loaf

Ingredients:

- ½ cup (60g) almond flour
- 1 ½ cups (180g) gluten-free 1:1 flour
- ¼ teaspoon (1g) baking soda
- 2 teaspoons (10g) baking powder
- ½ teaspoon (3g) ground cinnamon
- ¼ teaspoon (1g) ground nutmeg
- 1 cup (240g) mashed overripe bananas
- ⅓ cup (80ml) extra-virgin olive oil
- 2 large eggs
- ½ cup (100g) granulated sugar
- ¼ cup (60ml) milk (or milk alternative)
- 1 teaspoons (5ml) vanilla extract
- ¾ cup (90g) chopped walnuts, divided
- 3 tablespoons (15g) gluten-free oats for topping

Directions:

1. Preheat the oven to 350 °F (177 °C). Grease a loaf pan (9 x 5 inches) with cooking spray.
2. Add almond flour, gluten-free flour, baking soda, baking powder, cinnamon, and nutmeg into a bowl and stir well.
3. Add bananas, oil, eggs, sugar, milk, and vanilla into a separate bowl and whisk until smooth.
4. Combine the flour mixture and the banana mixture until no clumps remain.
5. Add ½ cup walnuts and fold gently.
6. Pour the batter into the loaf pan and top with oats and remaining walnuts.
7. Place the loaf pan in the oven on the center rack and bake at 350 °F (177 °C) for 40–50 minutes. A toothpick inserted into the center of the bread should come out clean.
8. Allow the bread to cool in the pan for 10 minutes before removing and transferring to a wire rack to cool completely.

Cheddar Sage Beer Bread

Yields: 1 loaf

Ingredients:

- 1 ½ cups (180g) gluten-free 1:1 flour
- ½ tablespoon (8g) baking powder
- 1 tablespoon (15g) granulated sugar
- ½ teaspoon (3g) dried sage
- ¼ teaspoon (1g) salt
- ¾ cup (180ml) gluten-free beer (lager works best)
- ½ cup (60g) freshly grated sharp cheddar cheese (or dairy free cheddar cheese)
- thinly sliced jalapeños (optional)
- 2 tablespoons (30ml) melted butter (or vegan butter)

Nut-Free, Egg-Free, Soy-Free

Directions:

1. Preheat the oven to 350 ºF (177 ºC). Grease a loaf pan with cooking spray.
2. Add flour, baking powder, sugar, sage, and salt into a bowl and stir.
3. Add beer and stir until smooth. Add cheddar cheese and jalapeño if using, and stir until well combined.
4. Scoop the batter into the prepared loaf pan and smooth the surface of the batter. Drizzle melted butter all over the surface of the batter.
5. Place the loaf pan in the oven and bake at 350 ºF (177 ºC) for 30–35 minutes.
6. Allow the bread to cool in the pan for 10 minutes before removing and transferring to a wire rack to cool completely.

Irish Soda Bread

Yields: 1 loaf

Ingredients:

- 1 ½ cups (360ml) buttermilk
- 5 tablespoons (70g) melted butter, divided
- 3 cups (360g) gluten-free 1:1 flour
- 1 teaspoon (5g) baking soda
- 2 teaspoons (10g) baking powder
- ¾ teaspoons (4g) salt
- 1 large egg
-

Optional mix-ins:
- Savory Soda Bread:
- garlic
- herbs
- shredded cheese
- sun dried tomatoes

Sweet Soda Bread:
- honey
- cinnamon
- raisins or other dried fruit
- apples

Directions:

1. Preheat the oven to 400 ºF (200 ºC) and arrange oven rack to the center position.
2. Beat eggs in a bowl, then add buttermilk and 3 tablespoons of melted butter.
3. Add flour, salt, baking soda, and baking powder into the bowl of a stand mixer.
4. Using the paddle attachment, set the mixer on low speed and mix until well combined.
5. Raise the speed to medium and pour in the egg mixture. Mix until you get a soft dough. If adding any mix-ins to make it a sweet or savory bread add them no, turn the mixer on a low speed until all ingredients are well distributed through the dough.
6. Once the dough is prepared, let it rest on the counter for 10 minutes.
7. Brush some of the remaining butter on the bottom and sides of a cast-iron skillet (about 8-10 inches).
8. On a well-floured surface form the loaf into a round disk shape about 2 inches thick and place the dough into the skillet. Slice an 'X' on the top of the dough 1 inch deep. Brush the top with remaining butter.
9. Place the skillet in the oven and bake at 400 ºF (200 ºC) for 30–40 minutes or until golden brown on top.

Savory Breakfast Bread

Yields: 1 loaf

Ingredients:

- ¼ cup (30g) gluten-free medium grind cornmeal
- 1 ¾ cups (210g) gluten-free 1:1 flour
- 1 tablespoon (15g) baking powder
- ¾ teaspoons (3g) dried thyme or any dried herbs of your choice
- ¼ teaspoon (1g) xanthan gum
- 1 teaspoon (5g) sea salt
- ¼ teaspoon (1g) ground black pepper
- ¾ cup (180ml) milk of your choice (dairy or non-dairy)
- 3 large eggs
- ½ cup (115g) butter, softened (or vegan butter)
- 1 ½ teaspoons (8ml) apple cider vinegar or fresh lemon juice
- 3 green onions, thinly sliced, or ½ cup chopped chives
- 2 cups (240) grated cheddar cheese, divided (or dairy free cheddar)
- 2 jalapeño peppers or poblano peppers, thinly sliced (optional)

Nut-Free, Soy-Free, Dairy-Free Option

Directions:

1. Preheat the oven to 350 ºF (177 ºC). Coat a loaf pan with cooking spray.
2. Add cornmeal, flour, baking powder, pepper, salt, herbs, and xanthan gum into a bowl and mix well.
3. Add eggs, softened butter, vinegar, and milk into another bowl and whisk well.
4. Make a cavity in the center of the flour mixture. Add the egg mixture to the cavity and mix until just combined.
5. Stir in the jalapeño peppers, green onions, and 1 ⅔ cups of cheddar cheese and mix until well incorporated, making sure not to over-mix.
6. pour the batter into the loaf pan and smooth the top with a wet spatula or knife. Sprinkle the remaining cheese on top of the bread.
7. Place the loaf pans in the oven and bake at 350 ºF (177 ºC) for 40 minutes or until golden brown on top.

Cheesy Bagels

Yields: 10–12 bagels

Soy-Free

Ingredients:

- 3 cups (360g) almond flour
- 2 tablespoons (30g) baking powder
- 5 cups (500g) shredded mozzarella cheese
- 4 large eggs, beaten
- 4 ounces (115g) cream cheese, cut into cubes
- sesame seeds or poppy seeds to top (optional)

Directions:

1. Preheat the oven to 400 ºF (200 ºC). Line a baking sheet with parchment paper.
2. Combine almond flour and baking powder in a bowl.
3. Place mozzarella and cream cheese in a microwave-safe bowl. Microwave on high for 2 minutes stirring halfway through. Remove from the microwave and let it cool for 5 minutes.
4. Add almond flour mixture and eggs into the bowl of cheese. Mix with your hands until the dough is formed. If the dough is too hard to mix, then heat it in the microwave for about 20 seconds.
5. Divide the dough into 10–12 equal parts. Roll each portion between your palms into a rope. Then press the ends of the dough together to form a bagel. Place them on the prepared baking sheet and top with sesame seeds or poppy seeds (optional).
6. Repeat with the remaining dough balls. Bake in batches if required.
7. Bake at 400 ºF (200 ºC) for about 10–15 minutes or until light golden brown on top and firm to the touch.

Brazilian Cheese Bread

Yields: 25–30 mini cheese breads

Ingredients:

- 2 large eggs
- 1 ⅓ cups (315ml) whole milk
- ⅔ cup (160ml) extra-virgin olive oil
- 3 cups (360g) tapioca flour
- salt to taste
- 1 cup (100g) grated parmesan cheese

Nut-Free, Soy-Free

Directions:

1. Preheat the oven to 400 ºF (200 ºC). Grease 2 mini muffin trays with some cooking oil spray.
2. Mix eggs, milk, oil, tapioca flour, and cheese until well combined. Now taste a bit of the batter and add salt accordingly (since the cheese has some salt).
3. Spoon the batter into the muffin cups until they are ¾ full.
4. Place the muffin pan in the oven and bake at 400 ºF (200 ºC) for 15–20 minutes, until light brown on top.

CHAPTER 3

Cookies, Brownies, & Bars

Oatmeal Raisin Cookies

Yields: 12-14 cookies

Ingredients:

- 1 1/4 cups (150g) gluten-free 1:1 flour
- 1 teaspoon (5g) salt
- 1 teaspoon (5g) baking soda
- 3/4 teaspoon (3g) cinnamon
- 1/2 teaspoon (2g) xanthan gum
- 2 large eggs
- 1 teaspoon (5ml) vanilla extract
- 1 cup (225g) unsalted butter softened (or vegan butter)
- 1 cup (200g) brown sugar lightly packed
- 1/3 cup (70g) granulated sugar
- 3 cups (360g) gluten-free rolled oats
- 1 ½ cups (180g) raisins

Soy-Free, Dairy-Free Option

Directions:

1. Position one rack in top third of the oven, one in the bottom third of the oven and preheat the oven to 325°F (165°C). Line2 cookie sheets with parchment paper.
2. In a bowl add gluten free flour, salt, baking soda, cinnamon, and xanthan gum and whisk together.
3. In a separate bowl cream together the softened butter, eggs, brown and white sugars, and vanilla until light and fluffy
4. Mix the dry ingredients in batches into the wet ingredients until just combined, there should be no clumps of flour.
5. Add the oats and raisins and mix with a spatula until everything is evenly distributed.
6. Using a 2 oz scoop or a large spoon, scoop out 12 balls of dough onto the prepared cookie sheet with about 1 inch between each cookie. get your hands wet and gently press onto the cookie to flatten them slightly. Bake the cookies for 12-14 minutes, rotating the tray halfway through the baking time. They should be golden brown around the edges and slightly pale in the center.
7. Allow them to cool for about 7-10 minutes before removing from the baking sheet and placing them on a wire rack to cool completely.

Classic Chocolate Chip Cookies

Yields: 36 cookies

Ingredients:

- 2 1/4 cups (270g) gluten-free 1:1 flour
- 1 teaspoon (5g) baking soda
- 1 teaspoon (5g) salt
- ¼ teaspoon (1g) xanthan gum
- 1 cup (225g) butter, softened (or dairy free butter)
- ¾ cup (150g) granulated sugar
- ¾ cup (150g) brown sugar
- 1 ½ teaspoons (8g) vanilla extract
- 2 large eggs, room temperature
- 2 cups (360g) semi-sweet chocolate chips (or dairy free alternative)

Soy-Free, Dairy-Free Option

Directions:

1. Position one rack in top third of the oven, one in the bottom third of the oven and preheat the oven to 375°F (190°C). Line 2 cookie sheets
2. In a bowl add gluten free flour, salt, baking soda, and xanthan gum and whisk together.
3. In a separate bowl cream together the softened butter, eggs, brown and white sugars, and vanilla until light and fluffy
4. Mix the dry ingredients in batches into the wet ingredients until just combined, there should be no clumps of flour.
5. Add the chocolate chips and mix until they are evenly distributed.
6. Using a 2 oz scoop or a large spoon, scoop out 36 balls of dough onto the prepared cookie sheet with about 1 inch between each cookie. get your hands wet and gently press onto the cookie to flatten them slightly. Bake the cookies for 12-14 minutes, rotating the tray halfway through the baking time. They should be golden brown around the edges and slightly pale in the center.
7. Allow them to cool for about 7-10 minutes before removing from the baking sheet and placing them on a wire rack to cool completely.

Vegan Birthday Cake Cookies

Yields: 24 cookies

Ingredients:

- 1 tablespoon (15g) ground flax meal
- 3 tablespoons (45ml) water
- ½ cup (115g) vegan butter
- ½ cup (100g) granulated sugar
- ¼ cup (50g) brown sugar
- 2 teaspoons (10ml) vanilla extract
- 1 ¼ cups (150g) gluten free flour
- ¾ teaspoon (4g) baking powder
- ½ teaspoon (3g) baking soda
- ¼ (1g) teaspoon salt
- 3 tablespoons (45g) vegan sprinkles

Soy-Free, Vegan, Dairy-Free

Directions:

1. Preheat the oven to 350°F (177°C) and prepare 2 cookie sheets with parchment paper. Combine flax meal and water in a small bowl, stir then set aside for about 5 minutes.
2. Using a stand mixer, beat the vegan butter, brown sugar, and white sugar together until creamy and smooth, about 2 minutes. Add in the flax mixture and vanilla extract and beat until well combined.
3. In a separate bowl whisk the flour, baking soda, baking powder, and salt until well combined. Add the dry ingredients to the wet ingredients and gently combine until a smooth dough forms with no clumps. Gently fold in the sprinkles until evenly distributed through the dough.
4. Use a 2 oz cookie scoop or a large spoon to make about 24 cookie dough balls on prepared cookie sheets with 1 1/2 inches between each cookie. Press each dough ball down slightly with the palm of your hand. Bake the cookies for 12-14 minutes or until the outer edges just start to brown. Remove from the oven and allow the cookies to cool on the pan for about 5 minutes before transferring them to a wire rack to cool completely.
5. Store in an airtight container (line the container with parchment paper or wax paper). They can last 2-3 days at room temperature, about a week in the refrigerator, or 2 months in the freezer.

Low-Carb Chocolate Chip Cookies

Yields: 16 cookies

Ingredients:

- 4 cups (480g) almond flour
- ½ teaspoon (3g) salt
- 1 teaspoon (5g) baking soda
- ½ cup (115g) butter at room temperature (or vegan butter)
- 6 tablespoons (90ml) honey
- 2 teaspoons (10ml) vanilla extract
- ½ cup (120g) almond butter
- 2 large eggs
- 2 cups (360g) semi-sweet chocolate chips (or dairy-free chocolate chips)
- flaky sea salt to garnish

Soy-Free, Dairy-Free Option

Directions:

1. Preheat the oven to 350 °F (177 °C). Prepare 2 large baking sheets with parchment paper.
2. Combine almond flour, salt, and baking soda in a bowl and stir.
3. Beat butter, almond butter, vanilla, egg, and honey in a bowl with an electric hand mixer or stand mixer until smooth. Add dry mixture to the wet ingredients and mix until just combined. Gently fold in chocolate chips.
4. Use a 2 oz cookie scoop or a large spoon to make about 16 cookie dough balls on prepared cookie sheets with 1 inches between each cookie. Press each dough ball down slightly with the palm of your hand. Sprinkle flaky salt over the cookies.
5. Bake at 350 °F (177 °C) for about 13–15 minutes or until golden around the edges.
6. Let the cookies cool on the baking sheet for 5–7 minutes. Place the cookies on a wire rack to cool completely.
7. Store in an airtight container. They can last for 3-4 days at room temperature, about 2 weeks in the refrigerator, or 3 months in the freezer.

Amaretti Cookies

Yields: 24 cookies

Ingredients:

- 3 cups (360g) blanched almond flour
- ⅔ cup (135g) granulated sugar
- 6 tablespoons (70g) confectioners' sugar, plus extra ¾ cup (90g) for coating
- 1/4 teaspoon (1g) salt
- whites from 2 large eggs
- ½ teaspoon (3ml) almond extract
- 24 whole raw almonds

Dairy-Free, Soy-Free

Directions:

1. In a medium size mixing bowl combine the almond flour, granulated sugar, 6 tablespoons of confectioners' sugar, and salt.
2. Add egg whites and almond extract to the dry ingredients and mix until a cohesive dough forms.
3. Remove the dough from the bowl, form it into a disk shape and wrap it in plastic wrap. Place the dough in the fridge to chill for 1 hour.
4. Preheat the oven to 325 °F (165 °C) and prepare 2 baking sheets with parchment paper.
5. Remove the dough from the fridge and use a 2-ounce cookie scoop or a large spoon portion out 24 cookies rolling them between your hands to form a ball. Roll each ball in confectioners' sugar until well coated then place them on the prepared cookie sheet about 1 inch apart.
6. Place a whole almond on top of each cookie and press the cookies to flatten slightly.
7. Place in the oven and bake for 25-30 minutes or until they crackle and turn golden brown underneath the sugar coating.
8. Remove from the oven and allow them to cool on the pan for 5 minutes.

Baci Di Dama Cookies (Italian Hazelnut Cookies)

Yields: 20 sandwich cookies

Ingredients:

- 2 cups (240g) hazelnut flour
- 1 cup (120g) gluten-free 1:1 flour
- 4 tablespoons (30g) cornstarch
- 1 cup (225g) cold unsalted butter or dairy-free butter, cut into small cubes
- 1 pinch of fine sea salt
- 2 teaspoons (10ml) vanilla extract
- ¼ teaspoon (1g) salt
- ⅔ cup (135g) granulated sugar
- 10 ounces (280g) dark chocolate (or dairy-free dark chocolate)

Egg-Free, Soy-Free, Dairy-Free Option

Directions:

1. Line 2 large baking sheets with parchment paper.
2. In a mixing bowl, combine both flours, corn starch, salt, sugar, and vanilla extract.
3. Scatter butter and cut it into the mixture with your hands. Knead the mixture into a smooth dough. Divide the dough into 40 1 inch balls and. Place them on the baking sheets and press down the cookies very slightly with the palm of your hand. Place them in the refrigerator for 1 hour. About 45 minutes in preheat the oven to 325 °F (165 °C) and arrange rack to center position.
4. Bake for 15-18 minutes or until slightly golden brown. Make sure they do not become dark golden brown. Bake in batches.
5. Remove the cookies from the oven and allow them to cool completely on the baking sheet.
6. In a glass bowl melt the chocolate in a double boiler or a microwave. Stir often while melting.
7. The cookies will be flat on one side. Spread melted chocolate on the flat side of one cookie. Cover with another cookie, with the flat side on the chocolate. Do this with all the cookies.
8. Now place them upright on a wire rack until the chocolate sets.
9. Store in an airtight container. They can last for 4–5 days at room temperature, about 2 weeks in the refrigerator, or 2 months in the freezer.

Peanut Butter and Banana Cookies

Yields: 18-24 cookies

Ingredients:

- 2 medium ripe bananas, mashed
- 2 eggs
- 1 teaspoon (5g) baking soda
- ½ teaspoon (3g) salt
- 1 cup (200g) granulated sugar
- 2 cups (500g) peanut butter
- 3 cups (450g) semi-sweet chocolate chips
- 2 teaspoons (10ml) vanilla extract

Dairy-Free Option

Directions:

1. Preheat the oven to 350 °F (177 °C). Line 2 large baking sheets with parchment paper.
2. Add peanut butter, sugar, salt, eggs, baking soda, and bananas into a large bowl. Mix well.
3. Add chocolate chips and fold gently.
4. Drop spoonfuls of the mixture on the prepared baking sheet, leaving a sufficient gap between the cookies.
5. Bake in batches for 9–12 minutes or until golden around the edges.
6. Let the cookies cool on the baking sheet for 5–7 minutes. Place the cookies on a wire rack to cool completely.
7. Store in an airtight container. They can last for 3 days at room temperature, a week in the refrigerator, or 2 months in the freezer.

Vegan Gingersnap Cookies

Yields: 12 cookies

Vegan, Soy-Free, Nut-Free

Ingredients:

- 1 ¼ cups plus 2 tablespoons (180g) gluten-free 1:1 flour
- ½ teaspoon (3g) ground ginger
- ¼ teaspoon (1g) ground cloves
- ½ teaspoon (3g) ground cinnamon
- 1 teaspoon (5g) baking soda
- ¼ teaspoon (1g) salt
- ½ cup (100) packed brown sugar
- ½ tablespoon (8g) chia seeds mixed with 1 ½ tablespoons (23g) of water
- 6 tablespoons (90ml) melted coconut oil
- 3 tablespoons (40g) raw sugar to dredge the cookies
- 2 tablespoons (30ml) molasses

Directions:

1. Preheat the oven to 350 °F (177 °C). Line 2 large baking sheets with parchment paper.
2. Add peanut butter, sugar, salt, eggs, baking soda, and bananas into a large bowl. Mix well.
3. Add chocolate chips and fold gently.
4. Drop spoonfuls of the mixture on the prepared baking sheet, leaving a sufficient gap between the cookies.
5. Bake in batches for 9–12 minutes or until golden around the edges.
6. Let the cookies cool on the baking sheet for 5–7 minutes. Place the cookies on a wire rack to cool completely.
7. Store in an airtight container. They can last for 3 days at room temperature, a week in the refrigerator, or 2 months in the freezer.

Thumbprint Cookies

Yields: 18-24 cookies

Soy-Free, Dairy-Free

Ingredients:

- 8 tablespoons (115g) unsalted butter (or dairy free butter)
- ¼ cup (50g) granulated sugar
- 1/4 cup (50g) light brown sugar, lightly packed
- 1 large egg at room temperature, separated
- 1 teaspoon (5ml) vanilla extract
- 1/4 teaspoon (1g) salt
- 1/4 cup (30g) almond flour
- 1 ⅓ cups (160g) gluten-free 1:1 flour
- ½ cup (60g) chopped pecans
- ½ cup (120g) jam, or fillings of your choice

Directions:

1. Beat the butter and sugars together until very light. Add the egg yolk, vanilla extract and salt and mix well.
2. Add both flours to the wet ingredients and mix until a cohesive dough forms.
3. Cover and place the dough in the fridge to chill for 1 hour.
4. Preheat the oven to 350 °F (177 °C). Line 2 baking sheets with parchment paper
5. Remove the dough from the fridge and portion 24-30 cookies rolling each between your hands to form a ball.
6. With a whisk, whip the egg whites until foamy.
7. Dredge the dough balls in the egg white, roll them in the chopped pecans, and place them on the cookie sheets flattening the balls slightly with your palm.
8. Bake the cookies for 8 minutes then remove them from the oven. Using a spoon, make an indentation in the center of the cookie. Return them to the oven and bake for another 4-6 minutes.
9. Remove the cookies from the oven and transfer to a wire rack to cool.
10. Once the cookies have cooled you can fill each with the desired jam or filling.

Mexican Coffee Brownies

Yields: 18 brownies

Nut-Free, Soy-Free

Ingredients:

- 2 cups (480ml) pumpkin puree
- 4 large eggs
- 2 teaspoons (10ml) vanilla extract
- ⅔ cup (160ml) cold brew coffee
- ¼ cup (60ml) unsalted butter melted (or vegan butter)
- 1 cup (200g) granulated sugar
- 2 cups (340g) semi-sweet chocolate chips
- 1 ½ cups (180g) unsweetened cacao powder
- 1 teaspoon (5g) baking soda
- 1 cup (120g) gluten-free 1:1 flour
- 2 teaspoons (10g) salt
- ½ teaspoon (3g) chili powder
- 2 teaspoons (10g) ground cinnamon

Directions:

1. Preheat oven to 350 °F (177 °C). Prepare a baking dish (9 x 12 inches) with cooking spray
2. Add all the ingredients into a mixing bowl and stir until well incorporated.
3. Spoon the batter into the baking sheet evenly and smooth the surface with a spatula or a knife.
4. Place it in the oven and bake at 350 °F (177 °C) for 25-30 minutes or until a toothpick inserted into the center comes out with just a few crumbs, no batter.
5. Allow to cool completely in the dish and cut into squares.

The Perfect Brownies

Yields: 9 brownies

Dairy-Free

Ingredients:

- 2/3 cup (110g) semi-sweet or dark chocolate chips (or dairy free chocolate chips)
- 5 tablespoons (75ml) coconut oil or avocado oil
- 2/3 cup (130g) granulated sugar
- 2/3 cup (80g) blanched almond flour
- ½ teaspoon (3g) baking powder
- 2 tablespoons (10g) unsweetened cocoa powder
- ¼ teaspoon (1g) kosher salt
- 1 teaspoon (5ml) vanilla extract
- 2 large eggs
- coarse sea salt to sprinkle on top

Mix-ins:

- 1/3 cup extra dairy-free chocolate chips or chopped nuts of your choice

Directions:

1. Preheat the oven to 350 °F (177 °C). Prepare a baking dish (6 x 12 inches) by greasing it with cooking oil spray.
2. Place 1/3 cup chocolate chips and oil in a small saucepan over low heat. Stir often until very smooth. Turn off the heat and let it cool for a few minutes.
3. Meanwhile, add egg and sugar into a bowl and beat with an electric hand mixer until pale yellow. You may need to beat it for 2–3 minutes.
4. Add flour, baking powder, cocoa, and salt into another bowl and stir until well combined.
5. Add the beaten egg mixture into the saucepan with slightly cooled chocolate and whisk until smooth. Add vanilla and whisk until well combined.
6. Add the flour mixture and fold gently until just incorporated.
7. Now add the mix-ins and fold gently. Pour the batter into the baking dish.
8. Bake at 350 °F (177 °C) for about 25-30 minutes or until set in the center. Do the toothpick test. The toothpick should have a few crumbs when the brownies are done.
9. Allow to cool completely before cutting into squares

Vegan Avocado Brownies

Yields: 18-20 brownies

Vegan, Soy-Free, Dairy-Free

Ingredients:

- 1 cup (240g) ripened avocado, chopped
- ½ cup (120m) pure maple syrup
- 1 cup (240g) almond butter
- 3 cups (720ml) almond milk
- 1 cup (100g) cocoa powder, unsweetened
- 2 tablespoons (30g) baking soda
- 2 cups (240g) gluten-free 1:1 flour
- ¼ teaspoon (1g) salt
- 1 cup (180g) dairy-free chocolate chips

Directions:

1. Preheat the oven to 350 °F (177 °C). Coat a large baking dish (13 x 9 inches) with cooking spray.
2. Add avocado, maple syrup, milk, cocoa, and almond butter into a blender or food processor and blend until smooth.
3. Sift flour and baking soda into a bowl and add it to the blender. Blend until you get a smooth batter.
4. Pour batter into the baking dish. Sprinkle chocolate chips on top and press them into the batter slightly with a spoon.
5. Bake at 350 °F (177 °C) for about 40 minutes or until set in the center. Cut into squares once it has cooled completely.

Lemon Bars

Yields: 16-18 brownies

Ingredients:

For the crust:

- ⅔ cup (160ml) coconut oil
- 2 teaspoons (10ml) vanilla extract
- ½ cup (160ml) honey
- 3 cups (360g) almond flour
- ½ teaspoon (3g) salt
- ⅔ cup (85g) coconut flour

For the filling:

- 8 large eggs at room temperature
- 1 cup (240ml) fresh lemon juice, strained
- 6 tablespoons (60g) tapioca flour
- 3 cups (600g) granulated sugar
- zest of 3 lemons, grated

Directions:

1. Preheat the oven to 350 °F (177 °C). Prepare a baking dish (9 x 13 inches) with cooking spray.
2. Add oil, vanilla, and honey into a bowl and whisk well for the crust.
3. Stir in the flours and salt. You will have a crumbly dough.
4. Scatter the dough in the bottom of the baking dish and spread it evenly all over the dish. Press it with the back of a measuring cup to get a smooth compact surface.
5. Bake at 350 °F (177 °C) for about 13–15 minutes or until the top is light golden brown and slightly more brown around the edges.
6. Crack the eggs into a bowl. Add sugar, lemon zest, and lemon juice and whisk until well incorporated.
7. Whisk in the tapioca flour until free from lumps.
8. Pour the mixture into the baking dish.
9. Bake at 350 °F (177 °C) for about 25–35 minutes or until it is set in the center.
10. Allow the bars to cool for an hour before transferring to the fridge to cool for 2 more hours. Cut into 2-3 inch squares.
11. Store the leftover bars in the refrigerator for up to a week.

Banana Chocolate Chip Breakfast Bars

Yields: 8 bars

Vegan, Soy-Free, Dairy-Free

Ingredients:

- ½ cup (120ml) almond butter or any other nut or seed butter
- 3–4 medium size bananas, mashed
- 2 cups (160g) gluten-free rolled oats
- 1 cup (180) chocolate chips

Directions:

1. Preheat the oven to 350 °F (177 °C). Place a sheet of parchment paper in a baking dish (8 x 8 inches).
2. Add nut butter, bananas, and oats into a bowl and stir until well combined.
3. Add chocolate chips and fold gently.
4. Spread the mixture in the baking dish.
5. Bake at 350 °F (177 °C) for about 25–35 minutes or until set in the center. Cut into bars after they cool completely.
6. Store the leftover bars in an airtight container at room temperature for 3 days or 10 days in the refrigerator. You can freeze them in freezer-safe bags for 6 months.

Chocolate Flax Crunch Bars

Yields: 20-24 bars

Vegan Option, Soy-Free, Dairy-Free Option

Ingredients:

- 4 cups (480g) gluten-free rolled oats
- 1 ½ (8g) teaspoons ground cinnamon
- 1 cup (160g) whole flax seeds
- ⅔ cup (110g) dried fruit like cranberries, cherries, or apricots
- 2 cups (240g) almond flour
- 1 teaspoon (5g) salt
- 2 cups (340g) chocolate chips (or dairy-free chocolate chips)
- 1 cup (140g) raw sunflower seeds
- 1 cup (240ml) honey (or maple syrup)
- 1 cup (240ml) melted coconut oil, cooled
- 2 teaspoons (10ml) vanilla extract

Directions:

1. Preheat the oven to 350 °F (177 °C). Place a sheet of parchment paper in a large baking dish (13 x 9 inches).
2. Add almond flour, oats, cinnamon, ground flaxseeds, salt, chocolate chips, dried fruit, and sunflower seeds into a mixing bowl and stir well.
3. Make a depression in the middle of the mixture. Add coconut oil, vanilla, and honey into the depression and mix well.
4. Place the mixture in the baking dish and press it down well. You can use the back of a measuring cup to do so.
5. Bake at 350 °F (177 °C) for about 22–25 minutes for chewy bars or 25–30 minutes for crunchy bars. Cut the bars after they cool completely. If you have made crunchy bars try cutting them while still warm or they may break while cutting.
6. Store the leftover bars in an airtight container at room temperature for 3 days or 10 days in the refrigerator. You can freeze them in freezer-safe bags for about 3 months but wrap each bar in plastic wrap before freezing.

Chocolate Dipped Coconut Macaroons

Yields: 18-20 cookies

Ingredients:

For plain macaroons:

- 3 large egg whites
- 1 teaspoon (5ml) vanilla extract
- 5 cups (240g) sweetened shredded coconut
- ¾ ()150g cup sugar

For chocolate macaroons:

- 1 cup (200g) chocolate chips, melted (or dairy free chocolate)
- ½ cup () cocoa powder

For dipping:

- melted chocolate (or dairy free chocolate)

Soy-Free, Dairy-Free Option

Directions:

1. Preheat the oven to 350 °F (177 °C). Place parchment paper on 2 large baking sheets.
2. Add egg whites, sugar, vanilla, and salt into a bowl and mix well. If you are making chocolate macaroons, add the melted chocolate (warm to the touch but not hot) and cocoa powder now. whisk until well incorporated.
3. Add shredded coconut and fold gently.
4. Scoop the mixture with a tablespoon or medium cookie scoop and drop it on the prepared baking sheets. Leave a sufficient gap between the cookies.
5. Bake at 350 °F (177 °C) for 15 minutes.
6. Remove from the oven and allow to cool completely on the baking sheets.
7. When cooled, dip the bottom half of each cookie in the melted chocolate. And place them back onto the cookie sheet. Allow chocolate to set before enjoying or storing in the refrigerator for later.

CHAPTER 4

Bread

4 in 1 Vegan Bread

Yields: 4 mini loaves / 1 loaf/ 2-3 pizza crusts / 4-5 dinner rolls

Ingredients:

- 2 cups (480ml) oat milk
- 1 cup (240ml) lukewarm water or more if required
- 2 tablespoons (30ml) fresh lemon juice or apple cider vinegar
- 1 ½ cups (180g) brown rice flour
- 1 cup (120g) arrowroot starch
- 1 ½ cups (180g) sorghum flour
- 2 cups (240g) gluten-free oat flour
- 4 tablespoons (60g) psyllium husk
- 4 tablespoons (20g) baking powder
- 1 ½ teaspoons (8g) salt
- 2 tablespoons (30g) granulated sugar

For toppings: Optional

- seeds of your choice
- dried herbs of your choice
- oats

Vegan, Nut-Free, Soy-Free, Dairy-Free

Directions:

1. Preheat Oven to 450 ° F (230° C).
2. Combine oat milk and lemon juice in a bowl. Keep it aside for about 10 minutes. This will be your buttermilk.
3. Combine all the flours, psyllium husk, baking powder, sea salt, and sugar in a mixing bowl.
4. Add buttermilk and stir lightly. Add about a cup of lukewarm water and stir until well combined. If the mixture is too dry, add more water, a tablespoon at a time and mix well each time.
5. Set aside the dough for 5 minutes.
6. To make mini loaves: Line 4 mini loaf pans with parchment paper. Divide the dough equally and place it in the loaf pans. Spread the dough evenly.
7. Scatter any of the optional ingredients on top.
8. Bake at 450 ºF (230° C) for about 15-20 minutes or until golden brown on top.
9. To make dinner rolls: Make the required quantity of dough and shape it into dinner rolls, as per your preferred shape and size. Scatter toppings if using. Place on a parchment lined baking sheet or dish and bake at 450 ºF for about 25 minutes. If at any time the top is getting too brown, turn the rolls over and continue baking.
10. To make a loaf: Grease a loaf pan (9 x 5 inches) with cooking spray. • Place the dough in the loaf pan. Scatter any toppings over the dough.
11. Bake at 450 ºF (230° C) for about 40–50 minutes.
12. To make pizza crusts: Line a baking sheet with parchment paper. Take the required quantity of dough as per your preferred size, flatten it to your preferred thickness, and place it on the baking sheet. You can bake as many crusts as you can on your baking sheet.
13. Bake at 450 ºF (230° C) for about 15 minutes. Spread pizza sauce and any toppings and bake for another 8–10 minutes.

Honey Oat Bread

Yields: 1 loaf

Soy-Free, Vegan Option, Dairy-Free

Ingredients:

- 2 1/3 cups 280g gluten-free 1:1 flour
- 2 1/2 (10g) teaspoons baking powder
- ¾ teaspoon (2g) xanthan gum
- 1 teaspoon (5g) salt
- 1 cup (95g) gluten-free rolled oats, divided
- 1 large egg or equivalent quantity of egg replacement
- 5 tablespoons (75ml) honey or maple syrup, divided
- ¾ cup (180ml) almond milk
- 1/4 cup (60ml) melted coconut oil
- 1 cup (240ml) plain Greek yogurt or dairy-free yogurt

Directions:

1. Preheat the oven to 350 °F (177 °C). Coat loaf pan (9 x 5 inches) with cooking spray.
2. Add flour, salt, and baking powder into a large mixing bowl and mix well.
3. In a separate bowl beat eggs, oil, yogurt, 3/4 cup oats and 3 tablespoons of honey.
4. Beat in the milk. Once the mixture is well combined and free from lumps, pour it into the flour mixture.
5. Mix well using a wooden spoon until just combined, making sure not to over-mix. You will have thick batter like dough.
6. Place dough in the prepared loaf pan, smooth the top, and scatter remaining oats on top of the dough.
7. Bake at 350 °F (177 °C) for about 30–40 minutes, until golden brown on top. Do the toothpick test. Cool for 10 minutes and take it out of the pan. Place on a wire rack to cool completely
8. Brush remaining honey over the top of the loaf. Slice and serve.
9. The bread will last for about 4 days at room temperature, a week in the refrigerator or 2 months in the freezer.

Artisan Dutch Oven Bread

Yields: 1 large boule

Nut-Free, Soy-Free, Dairy-Free, Vegan

Ingredients:

- 4 cups (500 grams) Caputo Brand, "Fioreglut", gluten-free flour
- 1 ½ teaspoons (5 grams) instant dry yeast
- 1 ½ cups + 3 tablespoons (400 grams) of luke-warm water, around 105°F
- 1 ½ teaspoons (10 grams) salt
- 3 teaspoons (12 grams) extra virgin olive oil (EVOO) plus more for mixing
- Some extra gluten-free flour for dusting

Directions:

1. In a large bowl add dry yeast to the flour, and add warm water. Mix to incorporate (before you mix, coat your hands with EVOO. If using a spatula to mix, coat the spatula with EVOO)
2. Now add the EVOO, and salt and continue kneading the dough with your hands• Once all ingredients are mixed thoroughly, let rest, covered with a damp kitchen towel for 10 minutes
3. After 10 minutes, coat your hands with some EVOO and shape the dough into a round shape.
4. sprinkle a bowl or proofing basket generously with gluten free flour and then place the dough in the basket.
5. Sprinkle some gluten free flour on top of the dough and cover with a kitchen towel until it doubles in size (typically 3 – 4 hours at room temperature).
6. Place a Dutch oven with its lid (or any other oven proof bakeware with a lid) into the oven and preheat the oven to 450 °F (230 °C)
7. Carefully remove the hot Dutch oven from your oven, and carefully place the dough inside. Score the top of the dough with a bread lame (or you can cut the top with a serrated knife) Place lid on top and cook in oven for 30 minutes with lid on
8. After 30 minutes, remove the lid and cook for 10 more minutes.
9. After 10 minutes, change setting on oven to broil and broil for 5 minutes (this will add a darker color to the top of the bread)
10. Remove the bread from the oven and allow the bread to cool for 5 minutes in the dutch oven then remove the bread and let it cool completely on a wire rack.

Sourdough Starter

Yields: 1 starter

Ingredients:

- Caputo Brand, "Fioreglut", gluten-free flour as required
- water, as required
- ½ tablespoon apple cider vinegar or more if required
- ½ teaspoon dry yeast or more is required

Directions:

1. **1st day:**
2. ½ cup Caputo Brand, "Fioreglut", gluten-free flour
3. ½ cup filtered water
4. Combine the water and flour in a large, non-metallic airtight container (a glass jar works well).
5. Add apple cider vinegar and yeast. Stir until you get a smooth, thick, sticky batter. Scrape the sides of the container to remove any dough. Cover the container loosely with plastic wrap. Place the container at constant room temperature at about 70 °F to 75 °F. Placing it on top of your refrigerator is a good way to maintain the temperature.
6. **2nd Day:**
7. Using the same quantity of flour and water as on the 1st day. Add water and flour into the container with the 1st day's starter and whisk well. Set it aside for 12 hours.
8. Repeat adding the flour and water after every 12 hours for the next 2–3 days until bubbles are visible in the mixture. When you see bubbles, the mixture is active. After 2–3 days, if you do not see many bubbles, add ½ tablespoon vinegar and whisk well. Check after 12 hours. If it is still not very active, add ½ teaspoon of yeast.
9. Repeat adding flour and water for another 2–3 days (7 days in all).
10. Each day try stirring the starter; the dough will be looser to the touch than the previous day. The starter is now ready and can be used to make sourdough bread. If you are making the bread on the 7th day, great; if not, you must maintain the starter for future use. Use as much starter as required for the bread recipe you are making, and maintain the remaining starter for future use if you plan to make it again within the next 6–7 days.
11. To maintain the starter: After the 7th day, dispose of half the starter and add the same amount of flour and water as the first day to the active starter, mix well, cover and set on the counter.
12. You must do this every day (dispose of half the mixture then add water and flour) until you want to make the sourdough bread.

Sourdough Bread

Yields: 1 loaf

Soy-Free, Nut-Free

Ingredients:

- 1 cup (125g) Caputo Brand "Fioreglut" gluten-free flour
- 2 tablespoons (16g) dry milk powder
- 2 tablespoons (16g) cassava flour or buckwheat flour
- 1 teaspoon (5g) baking powder
- ¼ teaspoon (1g) baking soda
- ½ teaspoon (3g) sea salt
- 1 large egg
- 2 tablespoons (30ml) olive oil
- ½ tablespoon (8g) psyllium husk powder
- ½ cup + 2 tablespoons (150ml) soda water
- 1 tablespoon (15ml) apple cider vinegar
- 2 tablespoons (25g) sugar
- 6 tablespoons (90g) gluten-free sourdough starter (see previous recipe)

Directions:

1. Stir together all the flour, milk powder, baking powder, baking soda, and salt in a bowl.
2. Before making the dough, ensure all the ingredients are at room temperature.
3. Add egg, oil, psyllium husk powder, apple cider vinegar, sugar, and sourdough starter into a mixing bowl. Stir until well combined and smooth, without lumps.
4. Add the dry ingredients and stir until well combined using a wooden spoon or a stand mixer with the paddle attachment.
5. Place a sheet of parchment paper in a large greased bowl. Dust the paper with some gluten-free flour.
6. Place the dough in the bowl. Sprinkle some gluten-free flour on top of the dough and finish off by brushing some olive oil on top of the dough. Cover the bowl loosely with plastic wrap.
7. Let the dough rise in the bowl for 2–3 hours at room temperature.
8. If you are baking the bread today, you can proceed to the next step . If you are baking the next day, place the covered bowl in the refrigerator overnight. Remove it from the fridge 2-3 hours before you are ready to bake it.
9. Preheat the oven to 400 °F (200 °C) and prepare a baking sheet.
10. lift the bread out of the bowl using the parchment paper that is lining the bowl and gently place it on a baking sheet. Brush some olive oil over the entire loaf.
11. Score the dough ball at a couple of places with a knife.
12. If you want a crunchy top, spray some water on the top of the dough and place it in the oven.
13. Spray the water over the bread every 15 minutes until the bread is baked. It should take about 60 minutes. When the bread is ready, the internal temperature of the bread should be 205 °F.
14. If after 60 minutes the crust is not dark enough you can switch the oven to broil mode for 5 minutes or until the desired color is achieved.
15. Remove the bread from the oven and cool it completely.
16. Slice and serve. You can store the bread slices in an airtight container at room temperature for about 3 days, 6–7 days in the refrigerator, or 2 months in the freezer.

Seeded Multigrain Sourdough Bread

Yields: 1 loaf

Ingredients:

For soaking:

- 3 tablespoons (18g) flax seeds
- 3 tablespoons (36g) red quinoa or tri colored quinoa, rinsed
- ⅓ cup (80m) water at room temperature
- 3 tablespoons (45g) gluten-free whole-rolled oats
- 3 tablespoons (30g) sunflower seeds

For the bread:

- 7 tablespoons (105g) gluten-free sourdough starter
- 3 tablespoons (45ml) pure maple syrup
- 2 ¾ cups (650ml) warm water (105 °F)
- 1 cup (160g) millet flour
- 2/3 cups (110g) tapioca flour
- 3 teaspoons (15g) fine sea salt
- 1 cup (140g) brown rice flour
- 1 ¼ cups (155g) gluten-free oat flour
- 3 tablespoons (30g) psyllium husk powder
- 2 tablespoons (30g) gluten-free whole-rolled oats

Egg-Free, Nut-Free, Dairy-Free

Directions:

1. For making gluten-free sourdough starter, refer to the previous recipe in this chapter.
2. Combine all the ingredients for soaking in a bowl. Cover the bowl and place it on your countertop for 6–8 hours.
3. Take a loaf pan (8 x 4 x 2 ½ inches) and line with parchment paper allowing extra paper overhanging from all sides.
4. To make the bread: Combine warm water, starter, and maple syrup in a large mixing bowl.
5. In a separate bowl combine all the flours, salt, and psyllium husk powder in a medium size mixing bowl.
6. Now add the flour mixture into the bowl with the starter mixture and stir using a fork. Keep stirring until it starts getting difficult to stir.
7. Mix in the soaked ingredients using your hands. Knead for about a minute. You will have a very sticky dough. You may need a bench scraper to scrape the dough off your hands. Let the dough rest for 10 minutes.
8. place the dough into the loaf pan. Moisten a rubber spatula or your hands with water (as often as required) and shape the dough at the top and edges. Make it sort of higher in the center and lower at the edges. You can do it by lifting the extra parchment paper and bringing it toward the center of the pans. Try to make the top smooth.
9. Keep the loaf pan covered with a moist kitchen towel. Allow the bread to rise at room temperature for 12–15 hours, depending on the temperature of your room. You will need to get the towel moist again a few times during the proofing process. It should rise to 1 ½ times its original size.
10. Preheat the oven to 550 °F (285 °C).
11. Score the dough at a couple of places on top with a knife. If you want a crunchy top, spray some water on the top of the dough. Scatter whole rolled oats on top.
12. Place the loaf pans in the oven and reset the temperature of the oven to 475 °F (245 °C). Bake for 55–60 minutes to be baked. The internal temperature should be 200–205 °F when the bread is ready.
13. Remove the bread from the oven and cool it completely.
14. Slice and serve. You can store the bread slices in an airtight container at room temperature for 3 days, 6–7 days in the refrigerator, or 2 months in the freezer.

Classic Sandwich Bread

Yields: 1 loaf

Soy-Free, Nut-Free

Ingredients:

- 3 cups (375g) Caputo Brand "Fioreglut" gluten-free flour
- 2 ½ teaspoons (9g) instant yeast
- 2 tablespoons (25g) granulated sugar
- 1 ½ teaspoons (8g) xanthan gum
- ¼ teaspoon (1g) cream of tartar
- 1 ½ cups (360ml) warm milk (95 °F)
- 1 teaspoon (5ml) apple cider vinegar
- toasted sesame seeds to top (optional)
- 2 teaspoons (10g) kosher salt
- 2 teaspoons (10ml) olive oil, plus extra to brush on top
- 2 egg whites at room temperature

Directions:

1. Prepare a loaf pan (8 x 4 x 2 ½ inches) and line with parchment paper.
2. Add flour, yeast, sugar, xanthan gum, and cream of tartar into the mixing bowl of a stand mixer and mix with a whisk until well combined.
3. Set the stand mixer on low speed with the paddle attachment. Add all the liquid ingredients into the bowl, one ingredient at a time, and mix well each time. Scrape the sides of the bowl whenever required.
4. Set the speed of the mixer to medium-high and mix until a smooth dough is formed. The dough will be moist and thick.
5. Place dough in the prepared loaf pans. Moisten a rubber spatula or your hands with water (as often as required) and shape the dough at the top and edges.
6. Grease a sheet of plastic wrap with some oil and use the wrap to cover the loaf pan. Place the loaf pan in a warm area until it is 1 ½ times its original size, about 45 minutes.
7. When the dough rises to slightly less than 1 ½ times its original size, preheat the oven to 375 °F (190 °C).
8. Remove the plastic wrap. Score the dough at a couple of places on top with a knife.
9. If you want to use sesame seeds, brush the top of the dough with some olive oil and scatter the seeds on top.
10. Place the loaf pans in the oven and bake for 45-60 minutes. When the bread is ready, the internal temperature of the bread should be 195 °F (90 °C).
11. Remove the bread from the oven and let it cool completely.
12. Slice and serve. You can store the bread slices in an airtight container at room temperature for about 3 days, about 6–7 days in the refrigerator, or 2 months in the freezer.

Focaccia Bread

Yields: 1 small loaf

Ingredients:

- 1 ¾ cups (210g) Caputo Brand "Fioreglut" gluten-free flour
- 1 teaspoon (2g) xanthan gum
- 1 ¼ teaspoons (3g) instant yeast
- ½ teaspoon (3g) salt plus extra to sprinkle
- 1 tablespoon chopped fresh herbs or 2 teaspoons dried herbs of your choice
- ½ tablespoon (5g) baking powder
- ½ tablespoon (6g) granulated sugar
- 1 cup (240ml) warm water (105°F / 40°C)
- ½ teaspoon (3g) apple cider vinegar
- 2 tablespoons (30ml) olive oil

Dairy-Free, Nut-Free, Soy-Free

Directions:

1. Combine sugar and warm water in a bowl.
2. Add flour, baking powder, yeast, xanthan gum, and salt into another bowl and stir until well incorporated.
3. Add the water mixture and mix with your hands or stand mixer fitted with the paddle attachment with the speed set on low.
4. Mix in the vinegar and oil. Keep mixing until you get a sticky dough.
5. Grease a large bowl with oil and scrape the dough into the bowl. Keep the bowl covered with a towel. Put the bowl in a warm place for about 30 minutes
6. Now preheat the oven to 400 °F (200 °C). Generously grease an 8x8 baking dish with olive oil.
7. Invert the bowl onto the baking dish so the risen dough falls into the baking dish. Flatten with your fingers to fit the shape of the baking dish.
8. Now with your fingers make depressions all over the dough
9. Generously brush olive oil over the dough. Scatter herbs and salt on top of the dough.
10. Place the baking dish on the top rack of the oven and bake for 20 minutes. If you want a golden brown top, broil for about another minute. Keep a watch, as it can burn quickly.
11. Slice the bread when it cools and serve.

Burger Buns

Yields: 6 buns

Ingredients:

- 1 cup (240ml) warm whole milk (104 °F / 40 °C)
- 2 tablespoons (25g) granulated sugar
- 1 teaspoon (5g) instant yeast
- 2 1/2 cups (300g) gluten-free 1:1 flour
- ½ teaspoon (3g) salt
- ½ teaspoon (3g) baking powder
- 2 large eggs, beaten
- 6 tablespoons (85g) butter, melted plus more for brushing
- 1 tablespoon (15ml) apple cider vinegar
- For toppings: Optional
- sesame seeds
- poppy seeds

Nut-Free, Soy-Free

Directions:

1. Combine sugar and warm milk in a bowl. When sugar dissolves completely, stir in the yeast. Cover and place the bowl in a warm area for about 10 minutes. It will be frothy.
2. Line a baking sheet with parchment paper. Grease the parchment paper with some cooking spray.
3. Combine flour, salt, and baking powder in a mixing bowl.
4. Using a wooden spoon, stir in the vinegar, egg, butter, and milk mixture. Beat constantly until you get a dough that is thick and sticky.
5. Make 6 equal portions of the dough using a scoop and place them on the baking sheet, leaving a sufficient gap between them.
6. With wet hands, give them a round shape. Loosely lay greased plastic wrap over the baking sheet. Place the baking sheet in a warm area for about 1 ½ hours or until they have nearly doubled in size.
7. Preheat the oven to 350 °F (177 °C). Brush egg wash on top of the buns. Scatter sesame seeds or poppy seeds on top if using.
8. Bake until golden brown on top, about 25–30 minutes.
9. After they come out of the oven, brush some melted butter on the hot buns.
10. Place the buns on a cooling rack and serve when fully cooled.

Jalapeno Corn Bread

Yields: 16 squares

Dairy-Free, Soy-Free, Vegan Option

Ingredients:

- 2 ½ cups (375g) cornmeal
- ½ teaspoon (2g) xanthan gum
- 1 ½ cups (180g) gluten-free 1:1 flour
- ⅔ cup (135g) light brown sugar
- 2 tablespoons (30g) baking powder
- 2 teaspoons (10g) salt
- 2 ⅔ cups (630ml) almond milk or any other milk alternative
- 1 cup (240ml) avocado or olive oil
- 4 large eggs, beaten, or 4 flax eggs
- ½ cup (60g) chopped jalapeño peppers

Directions:

1. Preheat the oven to 375 °F (190 °C). Generously grease a large baking dish (13 x 9 inches).
2. Add flour, xanthan gum, cornmeal, brown sugar, baking powder, and salt into a mixing bowl and stir until well combined.
3. Whisk in the milk, oil, and eggs. Keep whisking until well combined and free from lumps.
4. Add half the jalapeños and stir well. Pour the batter into the baking dish. Scatter remaining jalapeños on top.
5. Bake at 375 °F (190 °C) for about 35–40 minutes or until a toothpick inserted into the center of the bread comes out clean.
6. After the bread has cooled for at least 10 minutes, cut and serve. Store in an airtight container at room temperature for 3 days, in the refrigerator for 6–7 days, or freeze for about 2 months.

Drop Biscuits

Yields: 6 biscuits

Ingredients:

- 1 ¾ cups (210g) gluten-free 1:1 flour
- ½ teaspoon (3g) xanthan gum
- 1 ½ teaspoons (8g) cream of tartar
- 1 tablespoon (15g) baking powder
- ¼ teaspoon (1g) baking soda
- ¾ teaspoon (2g) kosher salt
- 2 teaspoons (10g) granulated sugar
- 8 tablespoons (115g) chilled butter cut into ¼" cubes (or vegan butter)
- 1 cup (240ml) cold milk (or milk alternative)
- 2 tablespoons (30ml) melted butter for brushing before baking (or vegan butter)

Nut-Free, Soy-Free, Dairy-Free Option, Vegan Option

Directions:

1. Preheat the oven to 425° F (220 °C). Prepare a baking sheet with parchment paper and arrange the oven rack to the center position. Cut 8 tablespoons of cold butter into 1/4" cubes and place back into the fridge until ready to use.
2. In a large mixing bowl whisk together gluten free flour, xanthan gum, baking powder, baking soda, salt, sugar, and cream of tartar together. Take the cold cubed butter out of the fridge and use a fork to cut the butter into the flour until pea size lumps form.
3. Make a well in the center of the dry ingredients and pour milk into the center of the well. Using a rubber spatula, mix the milk into the flour until a loose dough forms. make sure there are no clumps of flour at the bottom of the bowl. Work fast so the butter does not melt, you should still see small lumps of butter in the dough.
4. Using a 1/2 cup measuring cup lightly greased with cooking spray, scoop the dough onto a prepared baking sheet about 2 inches apart. Using a basting brush, lightly brush melted butter over each biscuit.
5. Place onto the center oven rack and bake for 15 minutes. Remove from the oven and allow to cool for about 5 minutes before serving.

Cheddar Bay Biscuits

Yields: 8 biscuits

Ingredients:

- 1 ¾ cups (210g) gluten free 1:1 flour
- ½ teaspoon (3g) xanthan gum
- 1 ½ teaspoons (8g) cream of tartar
- 2 teaspoons (5g) garlic powder
- 1 tablespoon (15g) baking powder
- ¼ teaspoon (1g) baking soda
- ¾ teaspoon (2g) kosher salt
- 2 teaspoons (10g) granulated sugar
- 8 tablespoons (115g) chilled butter cut into ¼" cubes (or vegan butter)
- 1 cup (240ml) cold milk or milk alternative
- 1 cup (115g) grated cheddar cheese or dairy free cheese
- 2 tablespoons (30ml) melted butter (or vegan butter) for brushing before baking

For garlic butter topping:
- 4 tablespoons (60g) butter, melted
- 2 tablespoons (30g) minced parsley
- 1 teaspoon (2g) garlic powder

Soy-Free, Nut-Free, Vegan Option

Directions:

1. Preheat the oven to 425 °C (220 °C). Prepare a baking sheet with parchment paper and arrange the oven rack to the center position. Cut 8 tablespoons of cold butter into 1/4" cubes and place back into the fridge until ready to use.
2. In a large mixing bowl whisk together gluten free flour, xanthan gum, baking powder, baking soda, garlic powder, salt, sugar, and cream of tartar together. Take the cold cubed butter out of the fridge and use a fork to cut the butter into the flour until pea size lumps form.
3. Make a well in the center of the dry ingredients and pour milk into the center of the well. using a rubber spatula, mix the milk into the flour until a loose dough forms. make sure there are no clumps of flour at the bottom of the bowl. Work fast so the butter does not melt, you should still see small clumps of butter in the dough.
4. Add shredded cheddar cheese and mix until just incorporated
5. Using a 1/2 cup measuring cup lightly greased with cooking spray, scoop the dough onto a prepared baking sheet about 2 inches apart. Using a basting brush, lightly brush melted butter over each biscuit.
6. Place onto center oven rack and bake for 15 minutes or until golden brown on the top
7. To make garlic butter topping: Add melted butter, garlic powder, and parsley into a small bowl and mix well.
8. Brush the garlic butter over the hot biscuits. Cool for at least 5 minutes and serve warm.

French Bread

Yields: 2 loaves

Ingredients:

- 2 tablespoons (30g) active dry yeast
- 3 teaspoons (15g) xanthan gum
- 1/2 cup (120g) superfine sweet rice flour
- 1 1/2 (180g) cups superfine white rice flour
- 1 cup (140g) tapioca starch
- 2 teaspoons (10g) sugar
- 1 1/2 teaspoons (9g) kosher salt
- 1 1/2 cups (360ml) warm water (105 °F / 40°C)
- 2 tablespoons (30ml) olive oil
- 2 large eggs, lightly beaten
- 2 teaspoons (10g) cornmeal (optional)
- 1 teaspoons (5ml) apple cider vinegar
- 2 tablespoons (30g) butter or vegan butter, melted

Nut-Free, Soy-Free, Dairy-Free Option

Directions:

1. Add sugar, yeast, and warm water into a bowl and stir until the sugar has dissolved.
2. Cover the bowl with plastic wrap and let the mixture rest for 6–10 minutes. It will turn frothy.
3. Add the rice flours, salt, tapioca starch, and xanthan gum into the bowl of a stand mixer. Fit the mixer with the paddle attachment and mix on low speed until well incorporated.
4. Add the yeast mixture, oil, vinegar, and eggs. Now set on high speed and mix for 3 minutes. Scrape the sides of the bowl if required.
5. Grease a baguette pan (with 2 molds for the bread) with some cooking spray. Dust each mold with cornmeal and place onto a baking sheet. You can also form the loafs onto a greased baking sheet if you don't have the baguette pans.
6. Divide the batter in two and scrape each portion into the molds. Using a greased spatula, give an oval shape to the batter. Score the top of the batter with a knife at 3–4 places. Cover the pan with a towel and place in a warm area for about 30 minutes or until it is double the original size.
7. Pour an inch of water into a baking dish and place it on the bottom rack in the oven. Preheat the oven to 400 °F (200 °C).
8. Brush melted butter on top of the loaves and place them in the oven on the center rack. Bake for 45 minutes or until golden brown on top. When the breads are ready, they should sound hollow when you tap them. Allow them to cool completely before slicing.

Dinner Rolls

Yields: 12–24 rolls

Nut-Free, Soy-Free, Dairy-Free Option

Ingredients:

- 3 ½ cups (420g) gluten-free 1:1 flour
- 1 ½ (8g) teaspoons salt
- 2 teaspoons (9g) instant yeast
- 1 ½ teaspoons (8g) xanthan gum
- 4 large eggs
- 4 tablespoons (60g) butter, softened (or vegan butter)
- 4 tablespoons (60g) honey
- melted butter to brush (or vegan butter)

Directions:

1. Mix flour, salt, yeast, and xanthan gum in a bowl.
2. Using a stand mixer, beat eggs, milk, and honey until well combined and light in color.
3. Add 2 cups of the flour mixture and the soft butter to the wet ingredients and mix on low speed until well combined.
4. Add remaining flour and mix well, scraping the sides of the bowl whenever required. Change the speed to high and beat until you get thick batter, free from lumps, around 3–4 minutes.
5. Keep the bowl covered for about an hour at room temperature.
6. Remove the batter's air bubbles by scraping the bowl's sides and bottom.
7. using a greased ½ cup, scoop the batter onto a baking sheet lined with parchment paper or into a greased muffin pan.
8. Cover the pans with plastic wrap and place in a warm area for about an hour to rise.
9. Preheat the oven to 350 °F (177 °C). Brush the risen rolls with butter and place them in the oven. Bake for 20-24 minutes or until golden brown on top
10. Once all the rolls are baked, allow them to cool for 10 minutes on the pan and then place on a wire rack to cool.
11. Wrap up any spare rolls that you don't eat. They'll stay good at room temperature for 2 days and for about 4-5 days in the refrigerator.

Rustic Kalamata Olive Bread

Yields: 1 large boule

Ingredients:

- 4 cups (500 grams) Caputo Brand, "Fioreglut", gluten-free flour
- 1 ½ teaspoons (9g) instant dry yeast
- 1 ½ cups + 3 tablespoons (400 grams) of luke-warm water, around (105°F / 40°C)
- 1 ½ teaspoons (9g) salt
- 3 tablespoons (20g) fresh rosemary, chopped
- 1 cup (150g) pitted kalamata olives, roughly chopped
- 1 tablespoon (15ml) extra virgin olive oil (EVOO) plus more for mixing
- Some extra gluten-free flour for dusting

Nut-Free, Soy-Free, Dairy-Free, Vegan

Directions:

1. In a large bowl add dry yeast to the flour, and add warm water. Mix to incorporate (before you mix, coat your hands with EVOO. If using a spatula to mix, coat the spatula with EVOO).
2. Now add the EVOO rosemary, olives, and salt and continue kneading the dough with your hands. Once all ingredients are mixed thoroughly, let rest covered with a damp kitchen towel for 10 minutes.
3. After 10 minutes, coat your hands with some EVOO and shape the dough into a round shape.
4. sprinkle a bowl or proofing basket generously with gluten free flour and then place the dough in the basket.
5. Sprinkle some gluten free flour on top of the dough and cover with a kitchen towel until it doubles in size, which is typically 3 – 4 hours at room temperature.
6. Place a Dutch oven with its lid (or any other oven proof bakeware with a lid) into the oven and preheat the oven to 450 °F (230 °C).
7. Carefully remove the hot Dutch oven from your oven, and carefully place the dough inside. Score the top of the dough with a bread lame (or you can cut the top with a serrated knife) Place lid on top and bake for 30 minutes with the lid on
8. After 30 minutes, remove the lid and cook for 10 more minutes.
9. After 10 minutes, change your oven setting to broil and broil for 5 minutes (this will add a darker color to the top of the bread)
10. Remove the bread from the oven and allow the bread to cool for 5 minutes in the dutch oven then remove the bread and let it cool completely on a wire rack.

Christmas Stollen

Yields: 2 loaves

Ingredients:

- 4 teaspoons (16g) active dry yeast
- 1 cup (240ml) warm milk (105 °F / 40 °C)
- ½ cup (100g) granulated sugar
- 1 ¾ cups (220g) fruit and peel mix
- 2 teaspoons (10g) xanthan gum
- ½ cup (60g) ground almonds
- 4 cups (480g) gluten free 1:1 flour
- zest of 2 lemons
- 8 tablespoons (112g) unsalted butter, melted plus extra to glaze
- 2 cups (300g) golden marzipan
- 4 large eggs
- 6 tablespoons (90g) powdered sugar or vanilla sugar to dust

Soy-Free

Directions:

1. Whisk together warm milk, yeast, and 2 tablespoons of sugar in a bowl. Cover the bowl with plastic wrap and let it rest for 5–8 minutes. It will become frothy.
2. In a large mixing bowl combine flour, remaining sugar, fruit and peel mix, xanthan gum, and ground almonds. Create a well in the center of the dry ingredients and add the milk mixture to the well along with the butter and eggs. Mix with a rubber spatula or your hands until you get a thick sticky dough with no clumps of flour.
3. Cover the dough with a damp kitchen towel and place the bowl in a warm area for about 60 minutes.
4. Place a sheet of parchment paper on your countertop. Dust it with flour then place half the dough on it and cover with another sheet of parchment paper. Roll with a rolling pin into a rectangle of about 12 x 10 inches. Peel off the top parchment paper. Repeat this process with the remaining dough.
5. Divide the marzipan into 2 equal parts. Roll each part with a rolling pin until it is about 11 x 5 inches.
6. Place 1 rolled marzipan in the center of each dough rectangle.
7. Fold the loaves in half lengthwise and pinch sides together to fully seal the marzipan in the dough. You can use the bottom parchment paper to assist in folding.
8. transfer the bread to a baking sheet keeping it on the parchment paper. You can use 2 smaller baking sheets if desired.
9. Bake at 350 °F (170 °C) for about 25 minutes until golden brown on top. Brush melted butter generously on top of the loaves. Place on a wire rack to cool to room temperature. Sprinkle powdered sugar on top of the loaves. Slice and serve.
10. These last for 3–5 days at room temperature in an airtight container, a week in the refrigerator, or about 2 months in the freezer.

Olive Tapenade Pull-Apart Bread

Yields: 1 loaves

Ingredients:

- 1 cup (125g) Caputo Brand "Fioreglut" gluten-free flour
- ½ cup (55g) grated parmesan cheese
- 1 tablespoon (15g) chopped fresh herbs of your choice plus extra to top
- 1 tablespoon (15g) chili garlic sauce
- 5 tablespoons (75g) olive tapenade
- 1/4 cup (60g) cold butter
- 6 tablespoons (90m) milk
- ½ teaspoon (3g) baking powder
- olive oil to drizzle
- melted butter to brush

Directions:

1. Place a sheet of parchment paper in a small loaf pan.
2. Add flour and baking powder into a bowl and mix well. Scatter the butter over the flour mixture and mix with a fork until only small pea sized lumps remain.
3. Add cheese and fresh herbs and mix until well combined. Mix in the milk until dough is formed.
4. Grease your hands with some oil and make small 2 inch balls of dough. Lay the balls on parchment paper. Drizzle olive oil over the balls and turn them so they are lightly coated in oil all over.
5. Place the balls in the loaf pan and press the balls slightly stacking them as you go. Brush chili garlic sauce and olive tapenade on top of the pressed balls. Scatter some fresh herbs on top.
6. Bake at 350 °F (177 °C) for 30–40 minutes, until light golden brown on top.
7. Cool for a few minutes then remove from the pan. Brush melted butter over the warm bread and serve.

CHAPTER 5

Cakes & Cupcakes

New York Cheesecake

Yields: 1 cheesecake (12 inches)

Soy-Free, Nut-Free

Ingredients:

For the crust:

- 1 ½ cups (180g) gluten-free graham crackers, crushed
- ¼ teaspoon (1g) ground nutmeg
- 2 tablespoons (25g) granulated sugar
- 4 tablespoons (60g) unsalted butter, melted

For the filling:

- 1 cup (200g) granulated sugar
- 2 tablespoons (15g) cornstarch or tapioca starch
- 1 ½ teaspoons (8g) vanilla extract
- 4 packages (8 ounces each) of cream cheese, softened
- 4 large eggs
- 1 cup (240ml) sour cream

For the sour cream topping:

- 4 tablespoons (25g) granulated sugar
- 1 cup sour (240ml) cream
- 1 teaspoon (5ml) vanilla extract

Directions:

1. Preheat the oven to 350 °F (177 °C).
2. **Crust:** Take a springform pan (12 inches) and wrap the bottom of the pan with heavy-duty aluminum foil.
3. Combine crushed graham cracker crumbs, nutmeg, and sugar in a bowl.
4. Stir in the butter. Transfer the mixture to the springform pan and press it well onto the bottom of the pan. Place in the fridge to chill until the filling is prepared.
5. **filling:** Beat sugar and cream cheese in a bowl using an electric hand mixer or a stand mixer until creamy.
6. Beat 1 egg at a time at medium speed, beating well each time.
7. Set the speed on high and beat in the cornstarch, vanilla, and sour cream. Beat until well incorporated.
8. Spread the filling on the crust and place the pan on a baking sheet.
9. Place the baking sheet into a preheated oven and bake for 35-45 minutes or until set.
10. **Sour cream topping:** Meanwhile, whisk the sugar, sour cream, and vanilla until smooth and well combined.
11. Remove the cheesecake from the oven and spread the sour cream topping all over the cream cheese layer. Place it back in the oven and bake for 15 minutes. Switch off the oven and let the cheesecake remain in the oven for an hour.
12. Let it cool to room temperature on your countertop then chill in the fridge for 4–6 hours before serving.

Classic Yellow Cake

Yields: 1 cake (8 inch) cake or 12-15 cupcakes

Ingredients:

- 1 ⅓ cups (160g) gluten-free 1:1 flour
- 1 ¾ teaspoons (9g) baking powder
- ¾ teaspoon (2g) xanthan gum
- 1 ⅓ cup (270g) granulated sugar
- ¾ teaspoon (5g) salt
- ¾ cup (170g) unsalted butter, softened (or vegan butter)
- 2 teaspoons (10ml) vanilla extract
- ¾ cup (180ml) milk or non-dairy milk
- 2 large eggs plus 3 egg yolks

Nut-Free, Soy-Free, Dairy-Free Option

Directions:

1. Preheat oven to 350 °F (177°C). Grease a round cake pan (8 inches) with cooking spray.
2. Combine flour, baking powder, salt, and xanthan gum in a mixing bowl.
3. In a separate bowl add sugar, vanilla, and butter and beat with an electric hand mixer or a stand mixer set on medium-high speed until well combined and smooth.
4. Add 1 egg at a time to the butter mixture and beat well each time until well combined.
5. Set the mixer on low speed and add milk, a little at a time until all the milk is mixed in.
6. Spoon the flour mixture into the wet ingredients a little at a time while the mixer is on low speed. Once all flour has been added, turn the mixer up to medium speed and beat until well combined about 2 minutes.
7. Spoon the batter into the prepared cake pan.
8. Bake at 350 °F (177°C) for 25-30 minutes or until a toothpick inserted into the center comes out clean.
9. Take the cake out and let it cool for 10 minutes in the pan. Invert the cake onto a rack and allow it to cool completely before slicing or decorating with a frosting of your choice.
10. With the same batter, you can make cupcakes as well. Simply pour the batter into greased or lined cupcake pans, filling up to ⅔, and bake for 20–22 minutes.
11.

Devil's Food Cake

Yields: 1 cake (8 inches) or 12–15 cupcakes

Ingredients:

- 1 cup (120g) gluten-free 1:1 flour
- 6 tablespoons (36g) dark cocoa powder, unsweetened
- ¼ teaspoon (2g) kosher salt
- ½ teaspoon (2g) xanthan gum
- 1 teaspoon (5g) baking soda
- ¾ cup (150g) packed light brown sugar
- 1 teaspoon (5ml) vanilla
- ⅔ cup (160ml) warm water
- ¼ cup (60ml) sour cream
- 4 tablespoons (60g) unsalted butter
- 1 large egg, beaten

Nut-Free, Soy-Free

Directions:

1. Preheat oven to 325 °F (165 °C). Grease a small, round cake pan (8 inches) with cooking spray. You can also use a muffin pan or cupcake pan with disposable liners to make cupcakes.
2. Add flour, cocoa, salt, xanthan gum, and baking soda into a mixing bowl until well incorporated.
3. In a separate bowl, beat the egg, butter, sugar, vanilla extract, and sour cream together until smooth. Add the warm water and mix again.
4. Pour the dry ingredients into the bowl with the liquid ingredients and mix with a rubber spatula until no clumps are present.
5. Spoon the batter into the baking pan or cupcake pan up to ¾.
6. Bake at 325 °F (165 °C) for about 25–30 minutes for cake or 20–22 minutes for cupcakes or until a toothpick inserted into the center comes out clean.
7. Take the cake or cupcakes out of the oven and allow them to cool for 10 minutes in the pan. Invert onto a rack and allow to cool completely before slicing or decorating with the frosting of your choice.

Red Velvet Cake with Cream Cheese Frosting

Yields: 1 cake (8 inches)

Ingredients:

- 2 ¼ cups (270g) gluten-free 1:1 flour
- ¾ tablespoon (11g) cornstarch or arrowroot starch
- ¾ teaspoon (4g) baking soda
- 1 teaspoon (5g) baking powder
- 1 ½ tablespoons (8g) cocoa powder
- 1 cup (240ml) buttermilk (or milk alternative + 1 tablespoon (15ml) lemon juice)
- ⅓ cup (75g) unsalted butter, softened (or vegan butter)
- ¾ teaspoon (4g) vanilla extract
- ¾ cup (180g) unsweetened applesauce
- 1 cup (200g) granulated sugar
- 1 teaspoon (5ml) white vinegar
- ¼ teaspoon (1g) salt
- 2 teaspoons (10ml) red food coloring (or 1 tablespoon (15g) of beet powder)

For the cream cheese frosting:

- ½ cup (120g) chilled cream cheese (or vegan cream cheese)
- 2 cups (250g) sifted powdered sugar
- ½ cup (115g) unsalted butter (or vegan butter)
- ½ teaspoon (3ml) vanilla extract

Vegan Option, Nut-Free, Dairy-Free Option, Soy Free

Directions:

1. Preheat oven to 350 °F (177 °C). Grease a cake pan (8 inches) with cooking spray.
2. Add flour, cornstarch, baking soda, baking powder, salt, and cocoa powder into a bowl and stir until well combined.
3. In a separate bowl add butter, sugar, apple sauce, and vanilla extract and beat until creamy and light. Stir in the red food coloring until fully incorporated
4. Add flour mixture and buttermilk, a little at a time, and beat until just combined.
5. Pour the batter into the prepared cake pan and bake at 350 °F (177 °C) for 30–35 minutes or until a toothpick inserted into the center comes out clean. Take the cakes out of the oven and allow them to cool for 10 minutes in the pan. Invert the cakes onto a rack. Let them cool completely before decorating.
6. Meanwhile, make the cream cheese frosting. Beat butter, cream cheese, and vanilla extract using an electric hand mixer until creamy. Beat in ½ cup of powdered sugar at a time until all sugar has been added and you have a light fluffy frosting.
7. Remove the cake from the oven and let it cool in the pan for 10 minutes. Invert the pan onto a wire rack and let it cool completely.
8. Cut the top off the cake to make it flat then cut the cake in half to make 2 layers.
9. Place a cake on a serving platter. Spread some frosting over the cake. Stack with the other layer of the cake. Spread the remaining frosting on top and sides of the cake.
10. Slice and serve. Store the leftover cake in an airtight container in the refrigerator. Use the cake within 5–6 days.

French Almond Cake

Yields: 1 cake (9 inches)

Soy-Free, Dairy-Free Option

Ingredients:

- 5 large eggs
- 1 ½ cups (300g) granulated sugar
- ¾ teaspoon (4ml) almond extract
- 2 ¾ cups (275g) almond flour
- ¼ teaspoon (1g) salt
- ½ cup (115g) unsalted butter, melted (or vegan butter)

For topping:

- 2 tablespoons (15g) powdered sugar
- ½ cup (60g) sliced almonds

Directions:

1. Preheat the oven to 350 °F (177 °C). Take a springform pan (9 inches) and coat it with cooking spray.
2. Crack the eggs into a bowl. Add sugar and beat with a whisk for 2 minutes.
3. Beat in the almond extract, almond flour, and salt. Beat until smooth.
4. Add butter and beat lightly.
5. Pour batter into the prepared cake pan and bake at 350 °F (177 °C) for 20 minutes. Remove the pan from the oven and sprinkle sliced almonds all over the top of the cake. Place the pan back in the oven and continue baking for 15–20 minutes or until a toothpick inserted into the center comes out clean.
6. Let the cakes cool completely in the pans at room temperature. Remove the cakes from the pans. Sprinkle powdered sugar on top.
7. Slice and serve. Place extra cake slices in an airtight container at room temperature for about 4 days or in the refrigerator for a week.

Pineapple Upside Down Cake

Yields: 1 large cake

Ingredients:

For the topping: (do this first)

- ½ cup (115g) butter melted (or dairy-free butter)
- ⅔ cup (135g) light brown sugar
- 2 cans (20 ounces each) of sliced pineapples
- maraschino or dark sweet cherries, as required

For the cake:

- ⅔ cup (150g) unsalted butter (or dairy-free butter)
- 2 cups (400g) granulated sugar
- 2 large eggs
- 2 teaspoons (10ml) vanilla extract
- 2 ⅔ cups (320g) gluten-free 1:1 flour
- 1 teaspoon (5g) salt
- 1 tablespoon (15g) baking powder
- 2 cups (480ml) milk (or milk alternative)

Soy-Free, Dairy-Free Option

Directions:

1. Preheat oven to 350 °F (177 °C). Coat a large baking dish (13 x 9 inches) with cooking spray.
2. Drizzle 4 tablespoons of melted butter all over the baking dish, take a pastry brush and brush it all over the baking dish.
3. Next, scatter brown sugar over the bottom of the baking dish. Lay the pineapple slices on top of the brown sugar. Place a cherry in the center of each pineapple slice and the gaps between each pineapple. Set it aside for now.
4. Add granulated sugar and butter to a bowl. Beat with an electric hand mixer until light and creamy.
5. Add 1 egg at a time and beat each egg well. Add vanilla extract and mix well.
6. Beat in the flour, baking powder, and salt. Once the mixture is well incorporated, add milk and beat until well combined. You will have a thick batter.
7. Scoop the batter into the baking dish on top of the pineapples. Spread the top of the batter with a spatula and make it smooth.
8. Bake at 350 °F (177 °C) for 50–60 minutes or until a toothpick inserted into the center comes out clean.
9. Let the cake cool for 20 minutes in the baking dish.
10. run a knife along the edges of the pan to make sure it isn't sticking in any spots. Invert the cake onto a large serving platter. Let the cake cool to room temperature.
11. Slice and serve. Place extra cake slices in an airtight container. Store it in the refrigerator for up to a week. Take it out of the refrigerator 15–20 minutes before serving, or you can even warm it slightly in the microwave for 15 seconds.

Carrot Cake

Yields: 1 small cake (8 inches)

Soy-Free, Dairy-Free Option, Vegan Option

Ingredients:

- 2 cups (240g) gluten free 1:1 flour
- ¾ tablespoon (11g) baking powder
- 1 teaspoon (5g) baking soda
- ¾ teaspoon (2g) ground cinnamon
- ½ teaspoon (2g) ground nutmeg
- ¾ teaspoon (2g) ground allspice
- ¼ teaspoon (1g) salt
- ¾ teaspoon (4g) vanilla extract
- ½ cup (60g) chopped walnuts
- ½ cup (60g) raisins
- 2 large eggs (or flax eggs)
- ⅓ cup (80ml) olive oil or unsalted butter, melted (or vegan butter)
- ⅓ cup (80ml) pumpkin puree
- ⅔ cup (160ml) coconut milk
- ¾ cup (90g) shredded carrot
- ½ teaspoon (3ml) apple cider vinegar
- 6 tablespoons (90ml) maple syrup

For cream cheese frosting:

- ⅔ cup (160g) cream cheese chilled (or vegan cream cheese)
- 1 ⅔ cups (330g) powdered sugar
- ⅔ cup (150) unsalted butter (or vegan butter)
- 2 tablespoons (30ml) milk (or milk alternative)

Directions:

1. Preheat the oven to 350 °F (177 °C). Grease 1 cake pan (8 inches) with cooking spray.
2. Add flour, baking powder, baking soda, salt, and all the spices into a bowl and mix well.
3. Combine milk and vinegar in a bowl and rest for 5–8 minutes. The milk will curdle slightly. This is your buttermilk.
4. Add the oil, milk, pumpkin, vanilla, eggs, and maple syrup to the dry ingredients and mix well. Stir in the carrots, walnuts, and raisins and mix well.
5. Pour batter into prepared cake pan and bake at 350 °F (177 °C) for 30–40 minutes or until a toothpick inserted into the center comes out clean.
6. Take the cake out of the oven and allow it to cool for 10 minutes in the pan. Invert the cakes on a wire rack and let them cool completely
7. Meanwhile, make the cream cheese frosting: Beat cream cheese, coconut milk, and butter in a bowl using an electric hand mixer until creamy. Beat in ½ cup of powdered sugar at a time until all the sugar has been used and a light fluffy consistency in achieved.
8. Slice the cake in half so you have two rounds of equal thickness. Place one round onto a serving platter cut side up and cover with a layer of frosting. Place the other round cut side down on top of the other and spread the frosting over the rest of the cake including the sides.
9. Slice and serve. Store the leftover cake in an airtight container in the refrigerator. Use the cake within 4–5 days.

Vanilla Cupcakes

Yields: 6 cupcakes

Ingredients:

For the cupcakes:

- ½ cup (115g) butter, softened (or vegan butter)
- 2 large eggs at room temperature
- 2 teaspoons (10ml) vanilla extract
- ½ cup (120ml) milk (or milk alternative)
- ¼ teaspoon (1g) salt
- ¾ cup (150g) granulated sugar
- 2 ½ teaspoons (12g) baking powder
- 1 ¼ cups (155g) gluten-free 1:1 flour

For the frosting:

- 1 teaspoon (5ml) vanilla extract
- ½ cup (115g) butter (or vegan butter)
- 2 tablespoons (30ml) milk (or milk alternative)
- 3 cups (360g) powdered sugar

Nut-Free, Soy-Free, Dairy-Free Option

Directions:

1. Preheat the oven to 350 °F (177 °C). Coat 6 cups of a cupcake pan with cooking spray or line them with disposable liners.
2. Add sugar and butter into a mixing bowl and beat using an electric hand mixer or stand mixer on medium speed until well incorporated.
3. Add eggs one at a time and beat until smooth.
4. Beat in the flour, baking powder, vanilla, and milk. Beat for about a minute.
5. Spoon the batter into the cupcake pan up to ¾.
6. Bake at 350 °F (177 °C) for 18–20 minutes or until the top is lightly browned and a toothpick inserted into the center comes out clean.
7. While the cupcakes are cooling, prepare the frosting.
8. Add butter and vanilla into a bowl and beat until well combined.
9. Add ½ of the powdered sugar and ½ of the milk and beat until well combined then add the rest of the milk and powdered sugar and beat until light and fluffy.
10. Once the cupcakes have cooled to room temperature spread the frosting on the cupcakes or pipe the frosting with a piping bag and serve.
11. Place extra cupcakes in an airtight container and store them in the refrigerator for up to a week. Take them out of the refrigerator 15–20 minutes before serving

Chocolate Cupcakes

Yields: 6 cupcakes

Ingredients:

For the cupcakes:

- 1 1/2 cups (225g) gluten-free 1:1 flour
- 1 cup (200g) light brown sugar
- ½ teaspoon (2g) salt
- ½ cup (40g) cocoa powder, unsweetened
- 1 ¼ teaspoons (6g) baking soda
- 1 egg, at room temperature
- 2 teaspoons (10ml) vanilla extract
- 2 tablespoons (30g) unsweetened applesauce
- 1 cup (240ml) milk (or milk alternative)
- ½ cup (120ml) vegetable oil or coconut oil
- 1 teaspoon (5g) white vinegar or apple cider vinegar

For the frosting:

- 6 tablespoons (85g) unsalted butter (or vegan butter)
- ½ cup (40g) cocoa powder, unsweetened
- 4 ½ tablespoons (67.5ml) milk (or milk alternative)
- 3 cups (360g) powdered sugar
- 2 teaspoons (10ml) vanilla extract

Dairy Free Option, Nut-Free, Soy Free

Directions:

1. Preheat the oven to 350 °F (177 °C). Coat a 6 cup cupcake pan with cooking spray or line it with disposable liners.
2. Combine cocoa, flour, salt, brown sugar, and baking soda in a mixing bowl.
3. Add egg, oil, milk, applesauce, vanilla, and vinegar and beat using a hand whisk until well incorporated.
4. Spoon the batter into the cupcake pan up to ⅔.
5. Bake at 350 °F (177 °C) for 22–24 minutes or until a toothpick inserted into the center comes out clean
6. While the cupcakes are cooling, prepare the frosting: Add butter, cocoa, and vanilla into a bowl and beat with an electric hand mixer starting on low speed then medium speed when the cocoa powder is mostly incorporated.
7. Add 1 cup of powdered sugar and 1 tablespoon of milk and beat well. Repeat this step until all the milk and powdered sugar have been used and the frosting is light and fluffy.
8. Once the cupcakes are fully cooled spread the frosting on the cupcakes or pipe the frosting with a piping bag and serve.
9. Place extra cupcakes in an airtight container. They can last a week in the refrigerator, or 3 months in the freezer. Take it out of the refrigerator 15–20 minutes before serving.

Peach Cupcakes with Bourbon Cream Cheese Frosting

Yields: 12 cupcakes

Ingredients:

For peach cupcakes:

- 1 1/2 cups (225g) gluten-free 1:1 flour
- ¾ teaspoon (4g) baking soda
- ¾ teaspoon (4g) baking powder
- ½ teaspoon (1g) xanthan gum
- ¼ teaspoon (1g) ground nutmeg
- ½ teaspoon (3g) salt
- ½ teaspoon (3g) cinnamon
- 2 tablespoons (30g) unsweetened applesauce
- ¼ cup (50g) packed light brown sugar
- ½ teaspoon (3ml) vanilla extract
- 1 ½ large peaches, peeled, cored, chopped
- 1 large egg, lightly beaten
- ¾ cup buttermilk or sour cream or full-fat yogurt
- ¼ cup (55g) unsalted butter, softened
- ¼ cup (50g) granulated sugar

For bourbon cream cheese frosting:

- ¾ cup (90g) powdered sugar
- ¼ cup (55g) butter
- ½ teaspoon (3ml) vanilla
- 8 ounces (225g) cream cheese
- 2 tablespoons (30ml) bourbon
- ½ teaspoon (1g) cinnamon

Nut-Free, Soy-Free

Directions:

1. Preheat the oven to 350 °F (177 °C). Coat 12 cups of a cupcake pan with cooking spray or line them with disposable liners.
2. Add flour, baking soda, xanthan gum, baking powder, salt, cinnamon, and nutmeg, into a bowl and mix well.
3. in a separate bowl beat together the applesauce, butter, granulated sugar, and brown sugar until creamy.
4. Beat the egg and vanilla into the applesauce mixture, followed by the buttermilk. Add about ½ cup of the flour mixture at a time and mix well each time until fully combined.
5. Finally, add the peach and fold gently.
6. Spoon the batter into the cupcake pan up to ⅔.
7. Bake at 350 °F (177 °C) for 18–22 minutes. Or until a toothpick inserted into the center of the cupcake comes out clean.
8. While the cupcakes are cooling, prepare the frosting: Add butter and cream cheese to a chilled bowl and beat with an electric hand mixer until creamy.
9. Add sugar, bourbon, cinnamon, and vanilla and beat well until the frosting is light and fluffy. Place the bowl in the refrigerator until ready to use.
10. Spread the frosting on the cupcakes or pipe the frosting with a piping bag and serve.
11. Place extra cupcakes in an airtight container. They can last for 5 days in the refrigerator or 3 months in the freezer. Take it out of the refrigerator 15–20 minutes before serving.

Lemon Lavender Cupcakes

Yields: 12 cupcakes

Vegan, Soy-Free, Dairy-Free

Ingredients:

For the cupcakes:

- 1 cup (120g) almond flour
- 1 cup (120g) gluten-free 1:1 flour
- ½ teaspoon (2g) salt
- ½ teaspoon (3g) baking soda
- ½ teaspoon (3g) baking powder
- 1 cup (200g) granulated sugar
- 1 large egg
- ½ cup (120ml) full-fat coconut milk or coconut cream
- 2 teaspoons (10ml) vanilla extract
- ½ cup (120ml) melted coconut oil
- ½ cup (120ml) fresh lemon juice, strained

For lavender icing:

- 1 cup (125g) powdered sugar
- 1 teaspoon (5ml) vanilla extract
- purple food coloring (optional)
- ½ cup (120ml) chilled coconut cream
- 1 ½ teaspoons (8ml) non-dairy milk
- ¼ teaspoon (2g) lavender extract

Directions:

1. Preheat the oven to 350 °F (177 °C). Coat a cupcake pan with cooking spray or line with disposable liners.
2. Add flour, baking powder, baking soda, and salt into a bowl and mix well.
3. Add sugar and coconut oil into another bowl and beat until well combined.
4. Beat in the lemon juice, egg, vanilla, and coconut milk into the coconut oil mixture.
5. Add wet ingredients into the flour mixture. Beat until the batter does not have any lumps.
6. Bake at 350 °F (177 °C) for 24–25 minutes. Or until a toothpick inserted into the center of the cupcake comes out clean.
7. While the cupcakes are cooling, prepare the frosting.
8. To make the frosting: Add coconut cream and powdered sugar into a chilled bowl and beat with an electric hand mixer until creamy.
9. Beat in the milk, vanilla, and lavender extracts. Beat in a few drops of food coloring, this is optional.
10. Spread the frosting on the cooled cupcakes or pipe the frosting with a piping bag and serve.
11. Place extra cupcakes in an airtight container. They can last for a week in the refrigerator, or 3 months in the freezer. Take it out of the refrigerator 15–20 minutes before serving.

Blueberry Buckle

Yields: 1 large cake

Ingredients:

For the cake:

- 4 cups (480g) gluten-free 1:1 flour
- 1 ½ cups (300g) granulated sugar
- 4 teaspoons (16g) baking powder
- 1 teaspoon (5g) salt
- 2 large eggs
- ⅔ cup (160ml) milk (or milk alternative)
- ½ cup (115g) unsalted butter, softened (or vegan butter)
- 2 teaspoons (10ml) vanilla extract
- 4 cups (480g) fresh or frozen blueberries

For streusel topping:

- ⅔ cup (130g) granulated sugar
- 2 teaspoons (4g) ground cinnamon
- ½ cup (115g) unsalted butter, softened (or vegan butter)
- 1 cup (140g) gluten-free 1:1 flour
- ¼ teaspoon (1g) salt

Nut-Free, Soy-Free, Dairy-Free Option

Directions:

1. Preheat the oven to 350 °F (177 °C). Coat a large baking dish (9 x 13 inches) with cooking spray.
2. For the streusel topping: Combine sugar, cinnamon, flour, and salt in a bowl. Add butter and mix until you get a crumbly mixture.
3. For the cake: Add flour, salt, and baking powder into a mixing bowl and stir well.
4. in a separate bowl beat the sugar, eggs, butter, and vanilla until well combined.
5. Add alternately some of the milk and some of the flour into the egg mixture and mix well each time.
6. After all of the flour and milk has been added, add blueberries and stir.
7. Add the batter to the baking dish. Scatter streusel topping over the batter,
8. Bake at 350 °F (177 °C) for 45–50 minutes. Or until a toothpick inserted into the center comes out clean.
9. Remove from the oven and allow to cool in the baking dish. Do not remove the cake from the baking dish. Cut into pieces and serve warm or at room temperature.
10. The cake will last for a week in the refrigerator, or 3 months in the freezer. Take it out of the refrigerator 15–20 minutes before serving.

Strawberry Cardamom Buckle

Yields: 1 large cake

Ingredients:

- 1 pound (450g) strawberries, sliced
- 1 1/3 cups (300g) unsalted butter (or vegan butter)
- 8 large eggs
- 4 teaspoons (20ml) vanilla extract
- 2 cups (400g) raw sugar plus extra to sprinkle
- zest of one lemon
- 3 1/3 cups (480g) gluten-free 1:1 flour
- 1 ½ teaspoons (8g) ground cardamom
- 1 teaspoon (5g) sea salt
- 1 teaspoon (5g) baking powder

To serve:

- whipped cream or vanilla ice cream (or dairy-free alternative)

Nut-Free, Soy-Free, Dairy-Free Option

Directions:

1. Preheat the oven to 350 °F (177 °C). Grease a large baking dish with cooking spray.
2. Place butter and sugar in the mixing bowl of a stand mixer. Fit the mixer with the paddle attachment. Beat until creamy.
3. Beat in 1 egg at a time, beating well each time. Add lemon zest and vanilla and beat until well combined.
4. Combine flour, cardamom, salt, and baking powder in a mixing bowl.
5. Add the flour mixture to the butter mixture and set the mixer on low speed. Beat until just combined.
6. Pour the batter into the baking dish. Place strawberry slices all over the batter. Scatter about 2 tablespoons of raw sugar all over the top of the cake.
7. Bake at 350 °F (177 °C) for 30–40 minutes or until golden brown on top. It may puff up in the center.
8. Remove from the oven and allow it to cool. Do not remove the cake from the baking dish. Cut into pieces and serve warm with whipped cream or vanilla ice cream.

Coffee Cake

Yields: 1 large cake

Ingredients:

For the topping:

- ⅔ cup (135g) brown sugar
- ⅔ cup (135g) sugar
- 2 teaspoons (10g) ground cinnamon
- 1 ½ cups (225g) gluten-free 1:1 flour
- 1 teaspoon (5g) salt
- 6 tablespoons (85g) unsalted butter, softened

For the cake:

- 4 cups (450g) gluten-free 1:1 flour
- 2 teaspoons (10g) baking soda
- 2 teaspoons (10g) baking powder
- 2 teaspoons (10g) ground cinnamon
- 1 cup (200g) brown sugar
- 1 cup (200g) granulated sugar
- 1 teaspoon (5g) salt
- 4 large eggs
- 4 teaspoons (20ml) vanilla extract
- 2 cups (475ml) buttermilk or non-dairy milk
- 1 cup (225g) unsalted butter or dairy-free butter

Nut-Free, Soy-Free, Dairy-Free Option

Directions:

1. Preheat the oven to 350 ° F (177 °C). Coat a large baking dish (9 x 13 inches) with cooking spray. Dust with flour as well.
2. To make the topping: Combine the sugars, cinnamon, flour, salt, and butter in a bowl and using a fork combine until you get a crumbly mixture.
3. To make the cake: Add flour, baking soda, baking powder, cinnamon, and salt into a bowl and mix well.
4. In a separate bowl beat the butter with an electric hand mixer until fluffy.
5. Beat in the vanilla, sugar, and brown sugar. Beat until well combined and smooth.
6. Add one egg at a time and beat well each time.
7. Add alternately some of the buttermilk and some of the flour mixture and mix well each time until well combined.
8. When you are done with adding all the flour and buttermilk, add the batter to the baking dish. Scatter the topping over the batter,
9. Bake at 350 °F (177 °C) for 45–50 minutes or until a toothpick inserted into the center comes out clean.
10. Remove the cake from the oven and place it on the rack to cool. Cut into pieces and serve warm or at room temperature.

Vegan Cheesecake

Yields: 1 cheesecake (6 inches)

Vegan, Dairy-Free

Ingredients:

For the crust:
- ½ tablespoon (8g) melted coconut oil
- 3 tablespoons (30g) almond flour
- 1 pinch of salt
- 1 ½ tablespoons (11g) granulated sugar
- 2 tablespoons (15g) gluten-free 1:1 flour

For the filling:
- ½ cup (65g) cashews, soaked in hot water for 15 minutes, drained
- ½ cup (100g) granulated sugar
- 1 ½ tablespoons (11g) cornstarch or arrowroot powder
- ⅔ cup (160g) silken tofu
- 4 tablespoons (60ml) lemon juice
- ½ teaspoon (3g) vanilla extract

Directions:

1. To make the crust: Preheat the oven to 350 °F (177 °C). Combine oil, sugar, flour, almond flour, and salt in a bowl. If the mixture is very dry add 1–2 teaspoons of vegan milk and mix well.
2. Take a small springform pan (6 inches). Place parchment paper on the bottom as well as the sides of the pan.
3. Transfer the mixture to the springform pan and press it well onto the bottom of the pan.
4. Bake at 350 °F (177 °C) for 10 minutes. Take it out of the oven and reset the temperature of the oven to 320 °F (160 °C).
5. To make the filling: Add drained cashews, sugar, corn starch, tofu, lemon juice, and vanilla into the food processor bowl or blender and blend until very smooth. Scrape the sides of the bowl, whenever required.
6. Spread the filling all over the crust using a spatula. Make sure the top is smooth.
7. Tap the springform pan lightly on your countertop 3–4 times so that any air pockets in the filling will come to the surface.
8. Bake until the top is golden brown. It will jiggle in the center. Let it cool to room temperature on your countertop. Remove the cheesecake from the pan. Chill for 4–6 hours in the refrigerator before serving.

CHAPTER 6

Tarts, Pies, Pastries & Cobblers

Pie Crust

Yields: 1 pie crust

Ingredients:

- 1 ½ cups (180g) gluten-free 1:1 flour
- 1 teaspoon (3g) xanthan gum
- ¼ teaspoon (1g) salt
- ½ cup (115g) cold unsalted butter or palm shortening, cut into cubes
- 4–5 tablespoons (60-75ml) cold milk (or milk alternative)

Egg-Free, Vegan Option, Dairy-Free Option

Directions:

1. Add the flour, xanthan gum, and salt into a bowl. Stir until well combined.
2. Add butter to the flour mixture and cut it into the mixture with a fork until the butter is cut into pea-size chunks.
3. Add milk and mix with your hands until well incorporated. If the mixture is too dry, add a teaspoon of milk and mix well each time until well combined. Shape the dough into a ball.
4. Place the dough over a sheet of wax or parchment paper. Place another sheet on top of the dough and roll with a rolling pin into a circle, slightly larger than the circumference of the pie pan. Peel off the top parchment paper.
5. Invert the pie pan on the dough. Now invert the entire thing, the pan, along with the dough. Now remove the parchment paper carefully. The dough will sit in the pie pan. Press the dough to fit inside the pan. If there are any cracks or holes while inverting, seal them by pinching the area. Cut any excess dough hanging over the edge of the pie pan and crimp the edges all around the pan.
6. You can bake the pie crust at 425 °F (220 °C) for about 7 minutes and then place the filling into the crust or bake the crust along with the filling.

Pop Tarts

Yields: 14–16

Ingredients:

- dough of 4 gluten-free pie crusts (See recipe on page 82)
- 2 tablespoons (20g) cornstarch or arrowroot powder
- 2 cups (240g) powdered sugar
- sprinkles to garnish
- 1 cup (240g) strawberry jam, pie filling, or any other filling of your choice
- 2 eggs beaten
- 8 teaspoons (40ml) milk

Nut-Free, Soy-Free

Directions:

1. Place a sheet of parchment paper on a large baking sheet.
2. Add jam and cornstarch into a small bowl and stir.
3. To make pie crust dough, refer to the previous recipe. Multiply the quantity of ingredients by 4 and make the dough for 4 pie crusts.
4. In step 4, as per the pie crust recipe, roll 1 dough ball into a rectangle about ⅛ to ¼ inch thick. Make 4–6 equal size rectangles from the dough. Repeat this process with the remaining 3 dough balls.
5. Place half the rectangles on the baking sheet. Spoon about 2 tablespoons of filling in the middle of each of these rectangles. Spread the filling slightly, leaving the edges bare.
6. Brush egg wash along the edges of the rectangles surrounding the filling.
7. Cover each with the remaining rectangles of dough. Press the edges to adhere. Crimp the edges with a fork.
8. Pierce a couple of holes on top of each pop tart. Brush the remaining egg wash on top of the tarts. Place the Pop-Tarts in the refrigerator for about 30 minutes. Preheat the oven to 400 °F (200 °C) while the poptarts are chilling.
9. Bake for 22–25 minutes or until golden brown. Let the tarts cool.
10. To make the glaze: Whisk together milk and powdered sugar in a small bowl. Pour the glaze over the tarts. Scatter sprinkles on top and wait for the tarts to cool to room temperature then serve.
11. You can store the extra tarts in an airtight container in the refrigerator for up to a week.

Chocolate Bourbon Pecan Pie

Yields: 1 pie

Ingredients:

- 1 unbaked pie crust (See recipe earlier in this chapter)
- 3 large eggs
- 1 cup (240ml) corn syrup light or dark
- 1/2 cup (100g) packed brown sugar
- 1/4 cup (60ml) melted unsalted butter (or vegan butter)
- 1/4 cup bourbon (60ml)
- 1/4 teaspoon (2g) salt
- 1 tablespoon (8g) cornstarch
- 2 cups (200g) pecans, chopped plus extra pecan halves for garnish.
- ½ cup (85g) dark chocolate chips (or dairy free chocolate)

Soy Free, Dairy-Free Option

Directions:

1. Make pie crust by following the recipe at the beginning of this chapter or use a store-bought gluten-free pie crust.
2. Preheat the oven to 425 °F (220 °C). Place pie crust in the fridge until the filling is prepared.
3. In a large mixing bowl combine the eggs, corn syrup, brown sugar, butter, bourbon, salt, and cornstarch together until well combined. Stir in the pecans and chocolate chips.
4. Take the pie crust out of the refrigerator and pour the filling into the crust. Place some pecan halves on top of the filling in the desired pattern.
5. Place the pie on a baking sheet and wrap the crust with strips of aluminum foil to prevent the crust from burning while baking.
6. Bake at 425 °F (220 °C) for 10 minutes then reduce the temperature of the oven to 350 °F (177 °C) bake for another 35-40 minutes. The center may jiggle slightly.
7. Remove from the oven and allow to cool for at least 1 hour before slicing and serving.

Brown Butter Pumpkin Pie

Yields: 1 pie

Ingredients:

- 1 unbaked gluten-free pie crust (See recipe earlier in this chapter)
- 6 tablespoons unsalted butter
- 2 eggs
- 1 can (15 ounces) of pumpkin puree
- 2 ½ teaspoons (4g) pumpkin pie spice
- 1/2 cup (100g) brown sugar
- 1 can (12 ounces) evaporated milk
- ½ teaspoon (2g) salt

Nut-Free, Soy-Free

Directions:

1. Preheat the oven to 425 °F (220 °C). You can use the pie crust recipe from earlier in this chapter or a store bought gluten-free pie crust.
2. In a heavy bottom skillet or saucepan, melt butter on medium high heat. Continue to cook until the butter is foaming and turns a brown color. Remove from the heat and stir in the brown sugar.
3. In a mixing bowl beat eggs. Add pumpkin, pumpkin pie spice, evaporated milk, and salt into a bowl and whisk until well combined.
4. When the butter mixture has cooled to a lukewarm temperature pour it into the mixing bowl with the other ingredients and mix well.
5. Pour the filling into the pie crust. Place the pie onto a baking sheet and wrap the edges of the crust in aluminum foil to prevent it from burning while baking.
6. Bake at 425 °F (220 °C) for 15 minutes. Turn the oven temperature down to 350 °F (177 °C) and continue baking for about 40-45 minutes or until the center doesn't jiggle.
7. Cool completely and chill for 4–6 hours. Slice and serve.
8. Store leftover pie in an airtight container in the refrigerator.

Dutch Apple Pie

Yields: 1 pie

Nut-Free, Soy-Free, Dairy-Free Option

Ingredients:

- 1 pie crust (see recipe at beginning of this chapter)
- 6 cups peeled, cored, thinly sliced apples, preferably Granny Smith apples
- 3/4 cup (150g) granulated sugar
- 2 teaspoons (5g) ground cinnamon
- ⅛ teaspoon (1g) salt
- 1 tablespoon (15ml) lemon juice
- ¼ cup (30g) gluten-free 1:1 flour
- ¼ teaspoon (2g) ground nutmeg

For the crumb topping:

- ½ cup (113g) unsalted butter (or dairy-free butter)
- ½ cup (100g) packed light brown sugar
- 1 cup (120g) gluten-free 1:1 flour

Directions:

1. Preheat the oven to 425 °F (220 °C). Prepare pie crust from the recipe earlier in this chapter or use a store-bought gluten-free pie crust.
2. To make the filling: Toss apples with lemon juice.
3. Mix the sugar, spices, flour, and salt in a bowl. Sprinkle this over the apples and mix well.
4. Spread the filling in the pie crust.
5. To make the crumb topping: Add butter, sugar, and flour into a bowl and mix until crumbly.
6. Sprinkle the crumb topping over the filling. Wrap the edges of the pie crusts with aluminum foil and place the pie pan on a baking sheet.
7. Bake at 425 °F (220 °C) for 30 minutes. Discard the foil from the crust. Place another sheet of foil loosely on top of the pie. Continue baking for another 20 minutes or until the crumb topping is golden brown or dark golden brown, depending on your preference.
8. Cool the pies on a rack for 2–3 hours.
9. Slice and serve. If you don't intend to finish the entire thing in a single day, you can place the leftover pie slices in an airtight container in the refrigerator for up to 4 days.

French Silk Pie

Yields: 1 pie

Ingredients:

- 1 baked gluten-free pie crust
- 4 large eggs
- 1 cup (226g) butter, softened
- 1 ¼ cups (250g) granulated sugar
- 4 ounces (113g) unsweetened chocolate, chopped
- 3 tablespoons (45ml) heavy cream
- 1 teaspoon (5ml) vanilla extract

For the whipped cream/garnish:

- 2 tablespoons (30g) powdered sugar
- chocolate shavings to garnish
- 1 cup (240ml) chilled heavy whipping cream
- 1 teaspoons (5ml) vanilla extract

Nut-Free, Soy-Free

Directions:

1. Preheat the oven to 425 °F (220 °C). You can use the pie crust recipe from earlier in this chapter or a store-bought gluten-free pie crust. Bake for 10 minutes or until the crust starts to turn golden brown.
2. Cool the baked crust.
3. Prepare a double boiler: Place a pot of water over high heat. When it starts boiling, turn down the heat to low. Place chocolate, eggs, and sugar in a heatproof bowl and place it in the double boiler. Whisk on and off until the mixture is smooth.
4. Whisk often until the mixture's temperature shows 160 °F on an instant-read thermometer.
5. Turn off the heat, place the bowl on the counter and let the mixture come to room temperature. Whisk on and off to speed up this process.
6. Add butter and vanilla, and heavy cream into a mixing bowl. Beat with an electric hand mixer or stand mixer until creamy and light, on medium speed.
7. Bring down the speed to low and beat in the melted chocolate mixture.
8. When all the mixture is added, beat on high speed for 5 minutes or until it becomes pale in color and increases in quantity.
9. Pour the filling into the crust and smooth the top with a knife. Keep the pie covered with plastic wrap and chill for 2–3 hours.
10. For whipped cream: Fix the mixer with a whisk attachment. Combine vanilla, heavy cream, and powdered sugar into a mixing bowl and set the mixer on high speed. Whip until stiff peaks are formed.
11. Spread the whipped cream over the filling or pipe the whipped cream using a piping bag. Scatter chocolate shavings on top.
12. Slice and serve. Place the remaining pie slices in an airtight container in the refrigerator. They can last for 3–4 days

Banana Cream Pie

Yields: 1 pie

Ingredients:

Filling:
- ½ cup (100g) granulated sugar
- 4 egg yolks
- 2 cups (480ml) milk (or milk alternative)
- 2 teaspoons (10ml) vanilla extract
- ¼ cup (30g) cornstarch or tapioca starch
- ¼ teaspoon (1g) salt
- 3 tablespoons (42g) unsalted butter (or vegan butter)

Crust and garnish:
- 2-3 bananas, sliced
- 1 baked gluten-free pie crust
- 1 container cool whip or coconut cool whip

Dairy-Free Option, Soy Free

Directions:

1. To make the filling: Add sugar, yolks, cornstarch, and salt into a saucepan and whisk until well combined.
2. Pour milk in a thin drizzle, whisking constantly while adding.
3. Put the saucepan over medium heat. Keep whisking until bubbles are visible. Continue cooking for 1–2 minutes after this point, whisking constantly. It will slowly thicken and coat the back of a spoon. When this happens, remove from the heat.
4. Add vanilla and butter and mix well. Allow the pudding to cool for about 15 minutes. Stir every 3–4 minutes.
5. Make the pie crusts following the recipe given at the beginning of this chapter or use a store bought gluten-free pie crust. Let the pie crust cool. Place half the sliced bananas at the bottom of the pie crust then pour half the filling on top of the sliced bananas. Spread the remaining bananas on top of the filling and then pour the rest of the filling over the bananas.
6. Cover the pies with plastic wrap and chill for 2 hours or until the pudding sets.
7. Decorate with cool whip and some banana slices

Chocolate Chess Pie

Yields: 1 pie

Ingredients:

- 1 gluten-free pie crust (using recipe earlier in this chapter or a store bought gluten-free pie crust)
- 1 ½ cups (300g) granulated sugar
- 2 large eggs
- 1 teaspoons (5ml) vanilla extract
- ¼ cup (60g) melted butter
- ¾ cup (180ml) evaporated milk
- 3 tablespoons (15g) cocoa powder
- To serve: (optional)
- whipped cream
- ice cream
- powdered sugar

Nut-Free, Soy-Free

Directions:

1. Preheat the oven to 375 °F (190 °C). You can use the pie crust recipe earlier in this chapter or use a store-bought gluten-free crust.
2. Add sugar and melted butter into a large bowl and whisk until smooth.
3. Beat in 1 egg at a time, beating well each time.
4. Add cocoa, evaporated milk, and vanilla and beat until well combined.
5. Spread the mixture over the pie crust.
6. Bake at 375 °F (190 °C) for 45 minutes or until the filling is set and does not jiggle.
7. Let it cool completely. Serve with any of the suggested serving options.

Puff Pastry

Yields: 8.8 ounces (1 sheet) of pastry

Ingredients:

- 1 cup (125g) gluten-free 1:1 flour plus extra for dusting
- ½ teaspoon (2g) xanthan gum
- 1 ½ tablespoons (21g) chilled unsalted butter, cut into cubes
- 3 ½ tablespoons (52ml) chilled water
- ¾ teaspoon (4g) caster sugar
- ¼ teaspoon salt (2 g)
- 6 tablespoons (84g) chilled butter, grated

Nut-Free, Egg-Free, Soy-Free

Directions:

1. Add flour, sugar, salt, and xanthan gum, into a bowl and stir until well combined.
2. Add butter and fut into the flour with a fork until fine crumbs are formed.
3. Add about a tablespoon of chilled water at a time and mix with a fork. Repeat this process until all the water is added. Add more water if required.
4. Knead gently just until it forms a dough. It may not be smooth right now but do not over-mix the dough. Otherwise, the butter will melt.
5. Keep the dough wrapped in plastic wrap and place in the refrigerator for around 25–30 minutes. If you have chilled it for more than 30 minutes, let it remain at room temperature for 5–8 minutes before you work with it.
6. Place a sheet of parchment on your counter and dust with flour. Place the dough on the parchment, flatten slightly, and place another sheet of parchment over the dough. Roll into a rectangle such that the length is around three times the width. It is alright if the dough cracks around the edges while rolling.
7. Remove the top sheet of parchment and sprinkle the grated butter evenly across the dough. Using the bottom parchment to assist, fold the dough like a letter. Lift ⅓ of the rolled dough from the long ends and fold it over itself towards the middle. Now lift the other side and place it over the folded dough. You will be left with 3 layers.
8. Turn the dough 90°. Roll the dough into a rectangle once again. Repeat the previous step of folding once again.
9. Wrap it tightly in cling wrap and place it in the refrigerator for at least 30 minutes.
10. The puff pastry is ready to be used. Use as suggested in any recipe that requires puff pastry.
11. Well-wrapped puff pastry (in plastic wrap) can last 7–8 days in the refrigerator or a month in the freezer.

Danish

Yields: 4 Danish pastries

Ingredients:

For Danish dough:
- 1 cup (120g) gluten free 1:1 flour plus extra for dusting
- 1 ⅛ teaspoons (5g) instant yeast or rapid-rise yeast
- ¼ cup (57g) butter or dairy-free butter, softened, cubed
- ¼ cup (50g) granulated sugar
- ⅛ teaspoon (1g) almond extract
- ⅛ teaspoon (1g) vanilla extract
- ½ teaspoon (2g) salt
- 6 tablespoons (90ml) milk or unsweetened almond milk
- 2 teaspoons (14g) of seedless raspberry (or any flavor) jam for each Danish
- 1 large egg

For the egg wash:
- ½ tablespoon (7g) water
- 1 large egg

For the glaze:
- 2 teaspoon water (10g)
- ¼ cup (25g) powdered sugar

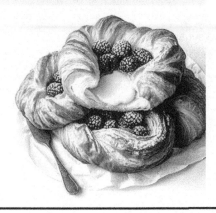

Soy-Free, Dairy-Free Option

Directions:

1. Add flour, instant yeast, and sugar into a freezer-safe bowl and stir.
2. Add butter cubes and cut them into the mixture using a pastry cutter or a fork until only pea size lumps remain.
3. Add milk, salt, vanilla, and almond extract, and egg into a bowl and whisk until well incorporated.
4. Add this into the bowl of the flour mixture and mix until well incorporated. You will get sticky dough.
5. Put the bowl in the freezer for about 25 minutes.
6. Dust a sheet of parchment paper with some flour. Put the dough over the paper. Flatten it slightly. Sprinkle some flour on top of the dough. Now fold the dough in half to form a semi-circle. Sprinkle some flour on the dough. Now fold it once again to form a quarter circle.
7. Now roll the dough into a circle with a thickness of about an inch.
8. Take a 3-inch circular cookie cutter and cut out circles from the dough. Place the cut-outs on a baking sheet lined with parchment paper.
9. Collect the scrap dough and reshape it into a ball. repeat steps 6-8. Repeat until all the dough is used up.
10. Using the back of a spoon create an indent in the center of each dough round. Place 2 teaspoons of jam in each indent.
11. For the egg wash: whisk together the egg and water in a small bowl and using a basting brush brush the egg wash over the exposed dough around the filling of the danish.
12. Bake at 400 °F (200 °C) for 18–20 minutes or until it turns golden brown.
13. Let the baked Danish cool on your countertop for around 20 minutes.
14. Make the glaze by whisking water and powdered sugar in a bowl. Trickle the glaze all over the Danish and serve.
15. Place unused Danish in an airtight container. They can last for about 3 days at room temperature or in the refrigerator for about a week

Café Au Lait Baked Beignets

Yields: 8 Beignets

Nut-Free, Soy-Free

Ingredients:

- ¼ cup (60ml) warm water
- 4 tablespoons plus 1 teaspoon (75g) granulated sugar
- 2 teaspoons (7g) active dry yeast
- 6 tablespoons (90g) coconut oil at room temperature
- 2 teaspoons (10ml) lemon juice
- 1 ¼ cups (300ml) milk, divided
- 4 large eggs, beaten
- 2 teaspoons (10ml) vanilla extract
- 1 cup (120g) coconut flour
- ½ teaspoon (3g) baking soda
- 2 teaspoons (10g) baking powder
- 1 teaspoon (5g) xanthan gum
- 2 cups (240g) gluten-free 1:1 flour plus extra for dusting
- ½ teaspoon (3g) salt
- 1 ½ teaspoons (2g) instant espresso or instant coffee
- 1–1 ½ cups (120-180g) powdered sugar

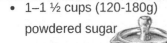

Directions:

1. Combine warm water, 1 teaspoon granulated sugar, and yeast in a small bowl. Let it rest for about 5–8 minutes.
2. Combine coconut flour, 1:1 flour, baking soda, baking powder, xanthan gum, salt, and remaining granulated sugar in a large mixing bowl.
3. Mix in the coconut oil with a fork. Mix until you get a crumbly mixture.
4. Mix yeast mixture milk, eggs, lemon juice, and vanilla into the bowl with the flour mixture. Stir until you get a thick, batter-like dough.
5. Keep the bowl covered in a warm area for an hour.
6. Preheat the oven to 400 °F (200 °C). Line 2 large baking sheets with parchment paper.
7. Dust your countertop with some flour. Place the dough on the floured area.
8. Knead the dough for 1 minute. Divide to dough into 2–3 portions
9. Roll each portion of dough into rectangles of about ¾ to 1-inch thickness.
10. Cut squares of 3 x 3 inches. Cut each square in half to make 2 triangles. If there is any scrap dough, collect it and reshape it into a ball. Roll again and cut into squares and then triangles.
11. Place the triangles on the baking sheets, leaving sufficient space between them.
12. Bake at 400 °F (200 °C) for 8–10 minutes or until it turns light brown around the edges. It should spring back when you press the beignets lightly.
13. To make café au lait glaze: Add ¼ cup milk and instant espresso into a bowl and stir until it dissolves completely. Stir in ½ cup of powdered sugar. Whisk until smooth. Add another ½ cup and whisk until smooth.
14. Drizzle the glaze over the beignets. Allow the glaze to set. It will look glossy.
15. Dust with remaining powdered sugar and serve.

Blueberry Hibiscus Hand Pies

Yields: 5 hand pies

Nut-Free, Soy-Free

Ingredients:

For the crust:

- 1 ¼ cups (150g) gluten-free 1:1 flour
- ½ teaspoon (3g) xanthan gum
- 6 tablespoons (85g) cold, unsalted butter
- 1 ¾ teaspoons (9ml) lemon juice or vinegar
- 1 tablespoon (13g) granulated sugar
- ½ teaspoon (3g) salt
- 1 large egg

For the filling:

- 1 ¼ cups (190g) fresh or frozen blueberries
- 1 hibiscus tea bag, blended
- 1 ¼ tablespoons (about 13g) gluten-free 1:1 flour or Clearjel
- 2 teaspoons (10ml) lemon juice
- ¼ cup (50g) granulated sugar
- 1 pinch of salt

For the topping:

- coarse sugar (optional)
- beaten egg for brushing

Directions:

1. For the crust: Add flour, xanthan gum, sugar, and salt into a bowl and stir until well combined. Cut the butter into the mixture until you get a crumbly consistency.
2. Add vinegar, egg, and lemon juice into another bowl and beat until frothy. Pour this mixture into the flour mixture and mix well. Press some of the mixture together between your fingers and see if the mixture is holding together. If it is crumbling away, add a tablespoon of cold water at a time and mix well each time until the mixture can hold together when pressed.
3. Flatten the dough into a rectangle and keep it wrapped in plastic wrap in the refrigerator for 1–3 hours.
4. Let the dough rest on the counter for 15 minutes at room temperature before making the hand pies.
5. Preheat the oven to 425 °F (220 °C). Prepare a baking sheet lined with parchment paper
6. Cook the berries in a saucepan over medium heat. Add hibiscus tea, sugar, salt, and ClearJel into the saucepan with the blueberries. Stir in the lemon juice. Stir often until the mixture is slightly thick.
7. Turn off the heat and let the berries cool completely.
8. Place a sheet of parchment paper on the counter and place the dough in the center. Roll the dough into a rectangle of around 7 x 17 ½ inches.
9. Cut the rolled dough into 10 equal squares or rectangles.
10. Distribute the squares onto the prepared baking sheet leaving a small gap between each.
11. Brush egg wash on the edges of 5 squares.
12. Distribute the filling equally over these 5 squares. Make a slit with a knife on each of the remaining 5 squares.
13. Now place each square with a slit over each berry-topped square. Press the edges to seal. Crimp the edges with a fork.
14. Brush the top of the hand pies with egg wash and bake at 425 °F (220 °C) for 18–20 minutes or until the crust turns light golden brown on top.
15. Cool until warm or room temperature and serve.

Apple Turnovers

Yields: 8-10 apple turnovers

Ingredients:

Nut-Free, Soy-Free, Egg-Free

For the filling:
- ¼ cup (50g) granulated sugar
- 1 tablespoon (10g) gluten-free 1:1 flour
- ½ teaspoon (3g) ground cinnamon
- 2 cups (240g) peeled, cored, chopped Granny Smith apples
- 17.3 ounces (2 sheets) gluten-free puff pastry dough
- 1 large egg (for brushing)

For the glaze:
- ¼ teaspoon (1g) vanilla extract
- ½ cup (60g) powdered sugar
- 1 teaspoon (5ml) milk or more as required

Directions:

1. Preheat the oven to 350 °F (177 °C). Place a sheet of parchment paper over a baking sheet.
2. Add flour, sugar, and cinnamon into a bowl and mix well. Stir in the apples.
3. The recipe for gluten-free puff pastry dough is given at the beginning of this chapter, you can also buy premade gluten free puff pastry sheets from most grocery stores.
4. Chop the rolled dough into 8-10 squares. Place around ¼ cup of the apple mixture on each of the dough squares (in the middle but not at the edges).
5. Brush the edges of each square lightly with egg wash. Now Fold the dough diagonally so a triangle is formed with the filling in the center. press the edges together and crimp with a fork.
6. Put them on the baking sheet lined with parchment paper. Cut a small slit into the top of each square and brush the outside with egg wash.
7. Bake at 350 °F (177 °C) for 22–26 minutes or until they are golden brown.
8. Meanwhile, make the glaze by mixing powdered sugar, vanilla, and milk in a small bowl.
9. Spoon the glaze over the cooled turnovers. Serve and enjoy.

Apple Fritters

Yields: 16–18 fritters

Ingredients:

- ⅔ cup (160ml) full-fat canned coconut milk
- 4 teaspoons (20ml) lemon juice or apple cider vinegar
- 4 large eggs
- 2 teaspoons (10ml) vanilla extract
- ⅔ cup (130g) brown sugar
- 3 teaspoons (6g) ground cinnamon
- 4 small apples, peeled, cored, diced (granny smith work best)
- 3 cups (360g) gluten-free 1:1 flour
- 4 teaspoons baking powder
- 1 teaspoon sea salt

For the glaze:
- ½ cup (120ml) milk alternative
- 2 cups (240g) powdered sugar

Nut-Free, Soy-Free, Dairy-Free

Directions:

1. Preheat the oven to 350 °F (177 °C). Place a sheet of parchment paper over a large baking sheet.
2. Beat eggs in a bowl, adding coconut milk, vanilla, and lemon juice.
3. Combine flour, baking powder, salt, sugar, and pumpkin pie spice in another bowl.
4. Add the flour mixture into the bowl of egg mixture and mix until you get a thick batter-like dough.
5. Scatter apples into the dough and mix well. Scoop about ½ cup of the batter and drop it on the baking sheet. Do this with all the batter, leaving a sufficient gap between the fritters.
6. Bake for 15–20 minutes at 350 °F (177 °C) or until they turn golden brown.
7. Meanwhile, make the glaze by mixing powdered sugar and milk.
8. Remove the turnovers and set the oven to broil mode.
9. Brush some of the glaze over the fritters. Place the baking sheet back in the oven and broil for a couple of minutes but keep an eye on the fritters as the glaze will burn easily if you aren't watching.
10. Cool until warm or room temperature then spoon the remaining glaze over the fritters. Let the fritters cool slightly before serving.

Italian Lemon Mascarpone Tart

Yields: 1 large tart

Nut-Free, Soy-Free

Ingredients:

- 1/2 cup (120ml) sour cream
- 3/4 cup (170g) chilled butter, cubed
- 1 cup (120g) gluten-free oat flour
- 1 ¼ cups (300g) mascarpone cheese
- 1 ¼ cups (300g) ricotta cheese
- 2/3 cup (130g) sugar
- 2 large egg yolk
- 2 large eggs
- 1/3 (90ml) of fresh lemon juice
- zest of 1 lemon

Directions:

1. In a mixing bowl add the oat flour and butter. Cut the butter into the flour using a pastry cutter or a fork.
2. Pour in the sour cream and mix until a dough forms.
3. Flatten the dough and keep it covered in cling wrap in the fridge for 20 minutes.
4. Preheat the oven to 400 °F (200 °C). Roll the dough into a circle to fit into a tart pan of about 10-12 inches in diameter.
5. Place the rolled dough in the tart pan and press it well onto the bottom and sides of the pan. Pierce holes all over the dough with a fork. Trim the edges of extra dough. Refrigerate for an hour.
6. Place something heavy on the dough, like dried beans or pie weights, and place it in the oven.
7. Bake at 400 °F (200 °C) until it turns light brown and dry in the middle. Remove from the oven and lower the temperature of the oven to 340 °F. Allow to cool while making the filling.
8. To make the filling: beat the mascarpone cheese and ricotta cheese together in a bowl until well combined. A stand mixer is very helpful for this.
9. Beat in the yolk, egg, sugar, lemon juice, and lemon zest until smooth.
10. Remove the weights from the crust and spoon the filling over the crust and place it back in the oven for 20–30 minutes, or until it sets on the sides and jiggles only slightly in the middle.
11. Cool completely and transfer it into the refrigerator. Cut into slices, and serve.

Dark Cherry Clafoutis

Yields: 6-8 servings

Nut-Free, Soy-Free

Ingredients:

- 1 pound (450g) dark cherries, stemmed and pitted (about 3 cups)
- 2 tablespoons (30ml) brandy or bourbon
- 3 tablespoons (45ml) melted and cooled butter, plus 1 teaspoon softened butter for the pan
- 3 large eggs
- ¼ cup (50g) granulated sugar
- ¼ cup (40g) super fine sweet rice flour
- ¼ cup (25g) blanched almond flour
- ¼ cup (25g) oat flour
- ½ teaspoon (2g) fine sea salt
- ¾ teaspoon (4g) vanilla extract
- ¾ cup (180ml) whole milk
- ¼ cup heavy cream (60ml)

To serve: Optional

- powdered sugar
- crème Fraiche
- whipped cream, sweetened

Directions:

1. Preheat the oven to 350 °F (177 °C). Grease a large cake pan or heavy bottom skillet with softened butter. Place the pan over a rimmed baking sheet.
2. Toss cherries with brandy in a bowl.
3. Beat the eggs in a bowl. Add the flours, salt, and sugar and whisk until well combined. Add vanilla, butter, heavy cream, and milk and mix well. You will have a thick batter.
4. Spoon the batter into the prepared baking pan. Scatter cherries on top of the batter. Spoon any liquid from the cherries over the batter.
5. Bake at 350 °F (177 °C) until golden brown on top or until a toothpick inserted into the center comes out clean.
6. Cool until warm. Sprinkle powdered sugar on top. Serve in bowls topped with crème fraiche or whipped cream if desired.
7. Put the remaining clafoutis into an airtight container in the refrigerator. They can last for about 8–10 days. Reheat and serve.

Pear Almond Tart

Yields: 1 tart

Ingredients:

Soy-Free

For the crust:

- 1 ¼ cups (160g) gluten-free 1:1 flour
- ½ teaspoon (2g) salt
- ½ cup (120ml) ice-cold water
- 1 stick (113g) unsalted cold butter, cut into cubes

For the filling:

- 1 can (8-ounces) almond paste, crumbled
- 2 tablespoons (30ml) melted butter
- 3 large Bosc pears, cored, cut into ½-inch thick slices
- 4 tablespoons granulated sugar (50g)
- 4 tablespoons (28g) powdered sugar
- 2 large eggs
- 1 tablespoon (15ml) fresh lemon juice, strained

Directions:

1. Add flour and cold butter to a bowl and cut the butter into the flour until only pea sized lumps remain.
2. add 2 tablespoons of water at a time to the flour mixture and mix between each until a dough forms. Make sure it is not sticky, it should be easy to work with.
3. Shape the dough into a ball. Now pat the dough into a disc and wrap it in plastic wrap. Chill for 1 hour or until the time you need to use it. You can make this dough a few days before preparing the tart, but keep it refrigerated. If you have chilled it for longer than an hour, place it on your countertop for about 10 minutes before using it.
4. Preheat oven to 350 °F (177 °C). Grease a small tart pan with a removable base (10-12 inches) with cooking oil spray.
5. Place the dough between 2 sheets of parchment paper and roll the dough into a circle about ¼ inch thick. The circle's diameter should be bigger than the diameter of the tart pan.
6. Peel off the top parchment paper. Now invert the dough onto the tart pan. Carefully move the dough into the tart pan and press it lightly onto the bottom and sides of the pan. Trim off excess dough. If there are any cracks in the dough, simply pinch the area to seal.
7. To prepare the filling: Place almond paste in the food processor bowl. Give short pulses until it breaks into smaller pieces. Blend in the egg, butter, and powdered sugar. Blend until smooth. Drizzle the mixture all over the tart crust.
8. Place the pear slices in a concentric manner over the filling. Brush lemon juice over the pears. Scatter granulated sugar all over the pear slices.
9. Bake for 20-25 minutes or until the filling is set. Allow the tart to cool completely, slice, and serve.

Roasted Red Pepper Tart

Yields: 1 tart

Nut-Free, Soy-Free

Ingredients:

For the crust:

- 1 ¼ cups (about 160g) gluten-free 1:1 flour
- ½ teaspoon (1g) salt
- ½ cup (120ml) ice-cold water
- 1 stick (113g) unsalted cold butter, cut into cubes

For the filling:

- 1 tablespoon (15ml) Dijon mustard
- 1 large egg
- ¼ teaspoon (1g) salt
- ⅛ cup (5g) torn fresh basil leaves
- ½ large white onion, chopped
- 3 roasted red bell peppers, roughly chopped
- ⅛ cup (8g) grated parmesan cheese
- ⅛ cup (30ml) heavy cream
- ¼ teaspoon (1g) ground black pepper
- 2 teaspoons (10ml) olive oil
- 2 cloves garlic, peeled, finely chopped

Directions:

1. Add flour and cold butter to a bowl and cut the butter in until pea-sized chunks. Add 2 tablespoons of water at a time to the flour mixture and mix between each until a dough forms. Make sure it is not sticky, it should be easy to work with.
2. Shape the dough into a ball. Now pat the dough into a disc and wrap it in plastic wrap. Chill for 1 hour or until the time you need to use it. You can make this dough a few days before preparing the tart, but keep it refrigerated. If you have chilled it for longer than an hour, place it on your countertop for about 10 minutes before using it.
3. Grease a small tart pan with a removable base (10-12 inches) with cooking oil spray.
4. Preheat the oven to 375 °F (190 °C). Place the dough between 2 sheets of parchment paper and roll the dough into a circle about ¼ inch thick. The circle's diameter should be bigger than the diameter of the tart pan.
5. Peel off the top parchment paper. Now invert the dough onto the tart pan. Carefully move the dough into the tart pan and press it lightly onto the bottom and sides of the pan. Trim off excess dough. If there are any cracks in the dough, simply pinch the area to seal. Place something heavy over the crust, like pie weights or dried beans, and place it in the oven. Bake at 375 °F (190 °C) for 10 minutes.
6. Take off the weights or beans and continue baking for another 5 minutes.
7. Meanwhile, beat the egg in a bowl with cream, basil, and seasonings.
8. Add oil to a pan and place it over medium-high heat. Add onion to the hot oil and cook until translucent and golden brown.
9. Stir in the garlic and cook for a minute. Add bell pepper and cook until peppers have slight charring on the skins. Turn off the heat.
10. Spoon Dijon mustard over the crust and spread it along the bottom. Scatter cheese over the crust.
11. Add the onion and bell pepper mixture to the egg mixture and pour into the tart shell. Make sure it is not filled right up to the top. It can spill out.
12. Bake for about 30–40 minutes or until the filling is set and golden brown.
13. Cool for a few minutes before removing from the pan.
14. Slice and serve.

Spinach and Cheese Tart

Yields: 1 small tart

Nut-Free, Soy-Free

Ingredients:

For the crust:

- 1 ¼ cups (160g) gluten-free 1:1 flour
- ½ teaspoon (2g) salt
- ½ cup (120ml) ice-cold water
- 1 stick (113g) unsalted cold butter, cut into cubes

For the filling:

- 2 tablespoons (30ml) pesto
- 2 large eggs
- ½ cup (120ml) sour cream
- 1 tablespoon (15ml) olive oil
- ½ cup (55g) grated parmesan cheese
- ½ cup (120ml) heavy cream
- ½ teaspoon (2g) ground black pepper
- ½ teaspoon (2g) salt
- 1 large onion, chopped
- 2 cups (200g) frozen spinach
- 4 cloves garlic, minced

Directions:

1. Add flour and cold butter to a bowl and cut the butter in until pea sized.
2. add 2 tablespoons of water at a time to the flour mixture and mix between each until a dough forms. Make sure it is not sticky, it should be easy to work with.
3. Shape the dough into a ball. Now pat the dough into a disc and wrap it in plastic wrap. Chill for 1 hour or until the time you need to use it. You can make this dough a few days before preparing the tart, but keep it refrigerated. If you have chilled it for longer than an hour, place it on your countertop for about 10 minutes before using it.
4. Preheat the oven to 375 °F (190 °C). Grease a tart pan with a removable base (10-12 inches) with cooking spray.
5. Place the dough between 2 sheets of parchment paper and roll the dough into a circle about ¼ inch thick. The circle's diameter should be bigger than the diameter of the tart pan.
6. Peel off the top parchment paper. Now invert the dough onto the tart pan. Carefully move the dough into the tart pan and press it lightly onto the bottom and sides of the pan. Trim off excess dough. If there are any cracks in the dough, simply pinch the area to seal. Place something heavy over the crust, like pie weights or dried beans, and place it in the oven. Bake at 375 °F (190 °C) for 10 minutes.
7. Take off the weights or beans and continue baking for another 5 minutes.
8. Beat the eggs in a bowl with sour cream, parmesan, cream, and seasonings.
9. Add oil to a pan and place it over medium heat. Add onion to the hot oil and cook until translucent and light golden brown.
10. Stir in the garlic and cook for a minute. Add spinach and mix well. Heat thoroughly. Turn off the heat.
11. Spread pesto over the crust.
12. Add the spinach mixture to the egg mixture and pour over the tart shell. Make sure it is not filled right up to the top. It can spill out.
13. Bake for about 30–40 minutes or until the filling is set and golden brown.
14. Cool for a few minutes before slicing.

Mixed Berry Crisp

Yields: 4 servings

Ingredients:

For the filling:

- 1 pound (about 450g) mixed berries, fresh or frozen, (about 3 cups)
- 1 tablespoon (8g) arrowroot starch or 1 ½ tablespoons (11g) cornstarch
- 1 tablespoon (15g) orange juice or lemon juice
- 3 tablespoons (45ml) honey or maple syrup
- 1/2 teaspoon (2g) grated orange zest or lemon zest

For the topping:

- ¼ cup (25g) packed almond flour
- 3 tablespoons (40g) packed brown sugar
- 3 1/2 tablespoons (50g) unsalted butter (or vegan butter)
- ½ cup (50g) gluten-free old-fashioned oats
- ¼ cup (30g) sliced almonds or chopped pecans (optional)
- ⅛ teaspoon (1g) salt
- To serve:
- dairy or dairy-free vanilla ice cream or whipped cream (optional)

Soy-Free, Egg-Free, Dairy-Free Option

Directions:

1. Preheat the oven to 350 °F (177 °C). Mix the berries, arrowroot, honey, orange juice, and zest into the baking dish (8 x 8 inches)
2. Combine all the topping ingredients in a bowl and mix until a crumbly texture forms.
3. Place spoonfuls of crumble mixture all over the berries.
4. Bake until golden brown on top, about 30–40 minutes. Cool for 10 minutes and then serve warm with ice cream or whipped cream (optional).

Strawberry Rhubarb Crisp

Yields: 4 servings

Ingredients:

For the filling:

- ½ pound (225g) fresh or frozen rhubarb, chopped into ½-inch pieces
- ½ cup (100g) granulated sugar
- 1 teaspoon (5ml) lemon juice
- ½ pound (225g) strawberries, halved or quartered depending on the size
- 3 tablespoons (about 30g) gluten-free 1:1 flour
- ½ teaspoon (3ml) vanilla extract

For the topping:

- ½ cup (60g) gluten-free 1:1 flour
- 1 teaspoon (3g) ground cinnamon
- ¼ cup (30g) chopped pecans or walnuts
- ¾ cup (150g) packed light brown sugar
- ½ cup (50g) gluten-free old-fashioned oats
- ½ teaspoon (1g) ground nutmeg
- ¼ cup (60ml) unsalted butter melted (or vegan butter)
- To serve:
- dairy or dairy-free vanilla ice cream or whipped cream (optional)

Soy-Free, Egg-Free

Directions:

1. Preheat the oven to 350 °F (177 °C).
2. Add strawberries and rhubarb into a mixing bowl and stir until well combined. Stir in sugar, lemon juice, vanilla, and flour. Grease a baking dish (8 x 8 inches) with cooking spray and spread the filling into the baking dish.
3. Combine all the topping ingredients in a bowl and mix until a crumbly texture forms.
4. Place spoonfuls of the mixture all over the filling.
5. Bake until golden brown on top, about 30–40 minutes. Cool for about 10 minutes.
6. Serve warm with ice cream or whipped cream (optional).

Bourbon Apple Crisp

Yields: 4 servings

Ingredients:

For the filling:

- 2 1/2 cups (300g) Granny Smith apples, cored, cut into ¼-inch thick slices
- ¼ cup (60ml) bourbon (or apple juice if you'd like an alcohol-free version)
- 1 teaspoon (4g) arrowroot starch or 1 ½ teaspoons (6g) cornstarch
- ⅛ teaspoon (1g) ground nutmeg
- 3 tablespoons (45ml) honey
- ½ tablespoon (8g) lemon juice
- ¼ teaspoon (1g) ground cinnamon

For the topping:

- ½ cup (50g)) gluten-free old-fashioned oats
- ¼ cup (30g) chopped pecans or walnuts (optional)
- 1 pinch sea salt
- ¼ cup (30g) firmly packed almond flour
- 3 tablespoons (30g) packed brown sugar
- 4 tablespoons (60ml) unsalted butter, coconut oil, or non-dairy butter melted
- To serve:
- vanilla ice cream or whipped cream (optional)

Soy-Free, Egg-Free, Dairy-Free Option

Directions:

1. Preheat the oven to 350 °F (177 °C).
2. Combine honey, bourbon, arrowroot, spices, and lemon juice in a small baking dish. Add apples and mix well. Spread the apple slices all over the dish.
3. Bake at until light brown on top, about 20 minutes.
4. In the meantime, add oats, pecans, salt, almond flour, brown sugar, and butter into a bowl and mix well.
5. Remove the baking dish from the oven and stir the apples. Spread the topping all over the apple filling. Bake again until the topping is golden brown. About 20 minutes
6. Cool for about 10 minutes. Serve warm with vanilla ice cream or whipped cream.

Peach Cobbler

Yields: 4 servings

Ingredients:

For the filling:

- 2 cups (300g) thinly sliced fresh peaches
- 3 tablespoons (45g) granulated sugar
- 1 tablespoon (8g) arrowroot starch or cornstarch
- ¾ teaspoon (2g) ground cinnamon

For the topping:

- 6 tablespoons (45g) gluten-free 1:1 flour
- 6 tablespoons (48g) almond flour
- 2 tablespoons (30g) granulated sugar
- ½ teaspoon (3g) baking powder
- 2 tablespoons (30g) milk (or milk alternative)
- 1 ½ tablespoons (22g) unsalted butter, cubed (or vegan butter)
- ¼ teaspoon sea salt

To serve: Optional

- whipped cream
- vanilla ice cream

Vegan Option, Dairy-Free Option, Soy-Free

Directions:

1. Preheat the oven to 400 °F (200 °C).
2. To make filling: You can use fresh or frozen peaches. If using frozen, thaw completely and drain all the liquid.
3. Cook peaches in a pan over medium heat until liquid is released. Bring down the heat to medium-low.
4. Stir in sugar, cinnamon, and cornstarch. Stir often until the sauce is thick and the peaches are cooked. Turn off the heat.
5. Spoon the peach filling into a baking dish.
6. To make topping: Add almond flour, sugar, baking powder, 1 :1 flour, and salt into a bowl and whisk well.
7. Cut the butter into the flour mixture until it has a crumbly texture.
8. Mix in the cold milk until well combined. Scoop the dough with a cookie scoop and drop it over the filling at different spots.
9. Place the baking dish onto a baking sheet and bake until golden brown on top, about 30–40 minutes. Serve warm with ice cream or whipped cream (optional).

Strawberry Balsamic Cobbler

Yields: 4 servings

Ingredients:

For the filling:

- 2 cups (300g) fresh strawberries, sliced
- 2 tablespoons (30ml) maple syrup
- 1 tablespoon (8g) gluten-1:1 flour
- 1 pinch of salt

For the topping:

- ½ cup + 1 ½ teaspoons (75g) gluten-free 1:1 flour
- ⅛ teaspoon (1g) baking soda
- 2 tablespoons (30g) maple syrup
- ⅛ teaspoon sea salt
- 3 tablespoons (45ml) melted coconut oil
- ½ teaspoon (2g) vanilla extract

To serve:

- Balsamic Glaze, for drizzling
- dairy-free ice cream (optional)
- dairy-free whipped cream (optional)

Vegan, Soy-Free, Dairy-Free

Directions:

1. Preheat the oven to 350 °F (177 °C)
2. To make the topping: Combine all the ingredients listed under topping in a bowl. You will get a thick and sticky dough.
3. To make filling: Combine all the ingredients listed under filling in a baking dish (8 x 8 inches). Make sure the mixture is well combined.
4. Scoop the dough with a cookie scoop and drop it over the filling at different spots.
5. Bake for 30-40 minutes or until golden brown on top. Remove from the oven and drizzle balsamic glaze lightly over the cobbler. Serve warm with ice cream or whipped cream (optional).

Pear & Fig Cobbler

Yields: 5 servings

Ingredients:

For the filling:

- 1 pound (450g) pears, peeled, cored, chopped
- 3-4 (120g) fresh figs sliced
- 1 tablespoon (8g) tapioca flour
- 1 teaspoon (2g) ground cinnamon
- ⅛ teaspoon (1g) ground cloves
- 1 teaspoon (5ml) vanilla extract
- 1 ½ tablespoons (23g) water
- 2 tablespoons (30g) granulated sugar

For the topping:

- 2 tablespoons (30g) granulated sugar
- ½ teaspoon (2g) ground cinnamon
- 1 cup (150g) gluten-free 1:1 flour
- ½ tablespoon (5g) baking powder
- 1 pinch of salt
- 3 tablespoons (45g) unsalted butter, melted (or vegan butter)
- 1 tablespoon (15ml) maple syrup
- ½ cup (120ml) whole milk (or milk alternative)

To serve:

- melted butter or vegan butter (optional)
- vanilla ice cream or dairy-free ice cream

Egg-Free, Nut-Free, Soy-Free, Dairy-Free Option

Directions:

1. Preheat oven to 350 °F (177 °C). Combine all the ingredients listed under filling in a bowl and stir until well combined. Spread the mixture in a baking dish (8 x 8 inches).
2. Combine flour, sugar, cinnamon, baking powder, and salt in a bowl.
3. Stir in the butter, maple syrup, and milk. Stir until a thick dough is formed.
4. Scoop the dough with a cookie scoop and drop it over the filling at different spots.
5. Bake for 30–40 minutes or until golden brown on top. Drizzle melted butter on the cobbler and serve warm with vanilla ice cream.

Plum and Amaretto Crumble

Yields: 8 servings

Ingredients:

For the topping:

- ¾ cup (150g) granulated sugar
- 1 ⅓ cups (200g) gluten-free 1:1 flour
- ¾ cup (170g) unsalted butter, cubed

For the filling:

- 2 pounds (900g) plums, halved, pits removed
- ½ teaspoon (2g) ground cinnamon
- 2 tablespoons (25g) brown sugar
- 4 tablespoons (60ml) amaretto liqueur
- To serve: Optional
- vanilla ice cream
- whipped cream

Egg-Free, Nut-Free, Soy-Free

Directions:

1. Preheat the oven to 350 °F (177 °C). Combine all the filling ingredients in a baking dish (9 x 13 inches). Spread the mixture evenly after combining.
2. To make the topping: Combine butter, flour, and sugar in a mixing bowl until crumbly in texture. Spread the topping all over the filling.
3. Bake until golden brown on top, about 30–40 minutes. Cool for about 10 minutes.
4. Serve warm with any of the suggested serving options.

Chocolate Raspberry Crumble

Yields: 8 servings

Soy-Free, Dairy-Free

Ingredients:

For the filling:

- 4 tablespoons (50g) granulated sugar
- 2 tablespoons (16g) tapioca flour
- 4 cups (500g) fresh raspberries

For the topping:

- ½ cup (40g) cacao, or cocoa powder
- 1 cup (100g) blanched almond flour
- 6 tablespoons (75g) granulated sugar
- ½ cup (120ml) coconut oil, melted
- ¼ cup (30g) pecans, chopped
- ½ cup (40g) shredded, unsweetened coconut
- ¼ teaspoon salt (1g)

To serve:

- vanilla ice cream or vegan vanilla ice cream
- chocolate fudge sauce or melted vegan dark chocolate

Directions:

1. Preheat the oven to 350 °F (177 °C). Coat a baking dish with some coconut oil.
2. Place raspberries in a bowl. Sprinkle sugar and tapioca flour over the raspberries and toss well. Spread the raspberries in a baking dish (7 x 11 inches).
3. Add all the ingredients listed under toppings into a bowl and stir with a fork until well incorporated.
4. Spread the topping mixture all over the raspberries.
5. Bake until golden brown on top, about 25–30 minutes. Cool for about 10 minutes. Serve warm with ice cream or melted chocolate (optional).

CONCLUSION

———— •●●●●●● ————

In conclusion, "The Simple Art of Gluten-Free Baking Cookbook" offers a delightful journey into the world of gluten-free baking, where satisfying your cravings for delectable snacks, breads, and desserts becomes an effortless and enjoyable experience. This cookbook has been carefully curated with a passion for flavor and a commitment to inclusivity, ensuring that everyone, regardless of dietary restrictions, can savor the pleasures of gluten-free treats.

Throughout these pages, you have discovered a diverse range of recipes that not only tantalize the taste buds but also cater to those with allergies and dairy-free requirements. By incorporating thoughtful alternatives and easy-to-follow instructions, we aimed to make your gluten-free baking adventure a seamless and rewarding one

I hope this cookbook has inspired you to embrace the simplicity and versatility of gluten-free ingredients. Whether you are an experienced baker or a novice in the kitchen, the recipes presented here empower you to create mouthwatering delights that rival traditional baked goods, if not surpass them.

Remember, gluten-free baking is an art that involves not only the right ingredients but also a dash of creativity and a whole lot of love. Embrace the process and let your culinary journey be a joyous one, filled with laughter, experimentation, and the satisfaction of sharing delightful treats with your loved ones.

As you continue to explore the boundless possibilities of gluten-free baking, always remember that the true essence of this art lies in its simplicity. Enjoy the magic of crafting delicious and allergy-friendly snacks, breads, and desserts, all while savoring the freedom to create dishes that cater to your unique tastes and dietary needs.

May this cookbook be a constant companion in your kitchen, inspiring you to create countless memorable moments and mouth watering delicacies. Happy baking, and may your gluten-free culinary endeavors bring you not only satisfaction but also the joy of sharing good food and cherished memories with those around you.

Here's to embracing the simple art of gluten-free baking and elevating your culinary experiences to new heights!

Andrew Rabbio

Made in the USA
Las Vegas, NV
17 April 2024

88798773R00063